From a French Country Kitchen

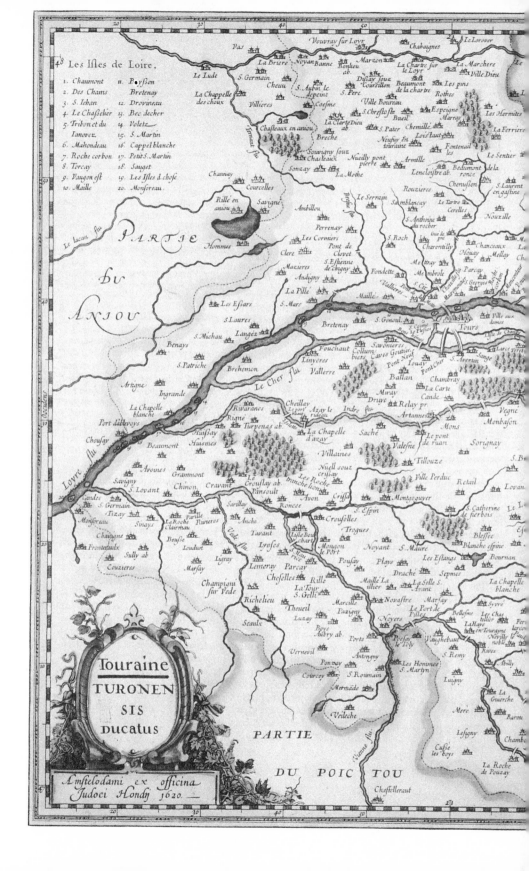

48 Les Isles de Loire,

1. Chaumont
2. Des Chams
3. S. Iehan
4. Le Chasselier
5. Tribon et du Ianovez
6. Mahondeau
7. Roche corbon
8. Torcay
9. Vauçon est
10. Maille

11. Boysson Bretenay
12. Drovineau
13. Bec decher
14. Voletz
15. S. Martin
16. Cappel blanche
17. Petit S. Martin
18. Sauget
19. Les Isles à chose
20. Monsoreau.

PARTIE DU ANJOU

Touraine

TURONENSIS
DUCATUS

Amstelodami ex officina
Judoci Hondij 1620.

PARTIE DU POICTOU

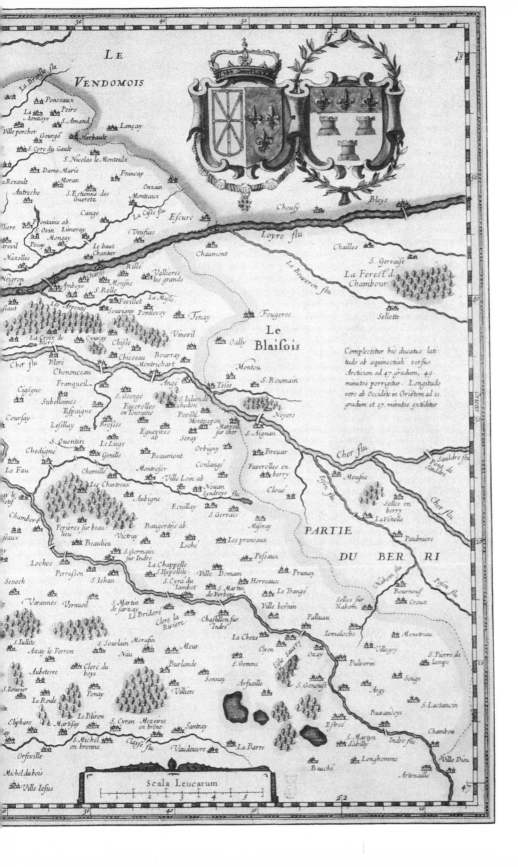

From a French Country Kitchen

The Culinary Tradition
of la Madeleine French Bakery & Café

Monique Esquerré and Patrick Esquerré

ISBN: 0-9643955-0-9

Published by la Madeleine French Bakery & Café

Translator: Maurice Elton
Food Photography: Matt Bowman
Food & Recipe Stylist: Kristine Ackerman, CCP
Illustrations: Martha McKibben
Book Design: Laura Lindgren

Manufactured in the United States of America
3 4 5 6 7 8 9 10

BIBLIOGRAPHY
Cuisine des Ardennes
Monique Esquerré
Editions Denoël, Paris

Les Salades Classiques et Raffinées,
Originales et Savoreuses
Gilbert Wenzler
Editions S.A.E.P., France

This book is dedicated to my husband, who for eighteen months exercised great patience while I worked weeks, weekends, even holidays, not only in my kitchen, which soon became too small, but also on the dining room table inundated with documents, notes, recipes, clippings bearing anecdotes, helpful hints, photographs, pie pans, and measuring cups.

My husband sometimes served as a guinea pig, sometimes had to picnic, for better or worse, at a hastily cleared corner, unhappily declaring to those around him, "My wife is writing a cookbook, while I am having to picnic on the run." Many times his mouth watered at the recitation of savory recipes which, alas, nourished only his gourmet mind.

And so I will make a promise to my patient husband who allowed me to help you appreciate French cuisine. I promise my husband to spoil him even more than before, to take great pains over every dish, which will be, in a very French way, a declaration of love.

—*Monique Esquerré*

I dedicate this book to my parents, who when I was young gave me a deep respect for freedom, for tenderness, and for the people who are part of my everyday life. I will always be grateful to them for allowing their children to live a dream every day without really knowing it.

In addition, I am dedicating this book to the associates who make up the la Madeleine family. They are really the heart of la Madeleine, and their achievements have made the bakeries what they are today.

This book is also dedicated to all people who do not have the opportunity to share the enjoyment, the wealth, the food of this world. Like many of our activities, this book will help us feed the hungry.

This book is also a way for me to say "Merci" to America, which helped my country during war and welcomed me when I journeyed to a new country to begin my dream anew.

—*Patrick Esquerré*

Kristine Ackerman
Sam Miller
Jim Henderson
Dr. Joe Goldstich

Maurice Elton
&
Cammie Vitale
&
Betty Cook

The La Madeleine Family
&
Stanley Marcus
&
Ray Herndon
&
Alain Bellet
&
French Tourist Office

Sue and Paul de Brantes
&
Philippe and Francoise Depée

Merci to the culinary artists and
friends who've shared not only
their recipes, but their valuable
time to make
this cookbook possible.

Mealtimes in my French homeland in the Château Country were special times, and they remain some of my fondest memories. From my early days as a young bride living in a small cottage to later days as mistress of Château les Pins, farm life gave us all a wonderful appreciation for fine food.

Dining was always a valued occasion for conversation and the exchange of ideas usually found in a devoted family. And thanks to the culinary talents of our nanny, Madame Henriette, who served our family so long she became one of its most-loved, most-appreciated members, these mealtimes also offered a wonderful opportunity to introduce the children to delicacies that might forever evoke happy childhood memories.

The kitchen always seemed to beckon not only the family, but friends alike, with the heart-warming comfort of home-baked breads, wonderful soups and stews—not to mention the most scrumptious desserts one can imagine.

My life has become simpler since those days at Château les Pins. However, one thing remains the same: the kitchen is still the center of our family gatherings.

For Patrick the memories of our country life and fresh country fare first prompted the founding of la Madeleine in America, which have come to serve as his and your home away from home.

Preparing healthy, delicious dishes for my family and friends has always been one of my greatest pleasures in life. Now I'd like to share our family's and our friends' favorite recipes and our way of life—a French country life that you can create and prepare in you own kitchen.

My greatest reward will be to hear that your family, and certainly your guests, have enjoyed these dishes, and that, in the tradition of Château Country and la Madeleine hospitality, these recipes from my France have served you well.

—Monique Esquerré

CONTENTS

INGREDIENTS OF A FRENCH COUNTRY HERITAGE

In my mind, I often look back upon the rich farm-lands that surrounded my family's home at les Pins, walk by the milk house that had been transformed into the cottage where I grew up, and recall the long, idyllic romps through the countryside with my brother Gérard. When we were very young, the country was still marked by the war: German armies had trampled the land and times were hard. I never realized it. There were vegetables growing in the garden, lambs and calves grazing on the hill-sides, and ducks, geese, and chickens scampering under our feet.

Even now, when I am usually so far away from the Loire Valley, I cannot escape those memories, nor would I wish to. And I go back as often as I can. I have blended those French ingredients into my new life in America and the life of la Madeleine Bakery & Café. During my childhood, my mother made sure that our table was always filled with the foods from the fields bursting with fresh flavor, and I have tried to do the same here in America.

Maman gave me my love for French country cooking, as well as a deep appreciation for nature and freedom. Her way of doing things has been passed down like an old family recipe from genera-tion to generation, and it has become a vital part of my family inheritance. She does what she does, family food, better than anyone I have ever known.

But her life at les Pins was not always easy. In the spring of 1940, when Monique had been engaged to François Esquerré for three years, she watched him ride away on horseback, the only mili-tary transport that the French army could muster against German tanks. She did not know if she

would ever see him again, and she almost didn't. After weeks of harrowing fighting, the Germans shot his horse out from under him and took him captive, marching him at gunpoint to a prison camp.

But he was not willing to be any man's pris-oner. While he was being marched to the prison camp, he took his chance when he saw that the guards were not watching. He leapt into a ditch and waited, not moving a muscle, until the German soldiers left. Walking by night, resting by day, he headed unswervingly for his beloved home at les Pins.

When he reached home, the first person he saw wore a German uniform and the first thing he heard was the dull staccato of gunfire on the second floor of his home. Château les Pins, once a Cister-cian monastery, was a beautiful limestone building with a commanding view of the surrounding countryside. Naturally, the German army seized it for their headquarters. The German soldiers swept into the house and its thirty rooms with unwar-ranted crudeness. When François arrived, they were using the Louis XV mirrors on the second floor for target practice.

François hid in the hayloft of a neighboring farmer's barn, watching the German troops and wondering when—or if—he would ever see Monique again. Three weeks later, he awoke one morning to find the château abandoned. The Ger-mans, for whatever reason, had departed, leaving only some soldiers in the area to guard their French prisoners who worked the fields. France had fallen, but François was still alive—and within the week, Monique had returned to his arms, where she would stay for the rest of their lives. Her laughter and her love returned the brightness to les Pins.

On a September afternoon in 1940, a gentle rain caressed the countryside as François took Monique as his wife in the small chapel beside the château. Monique looked up at the overcast skies and remembered an old French maxim: "When it rains on the day of a wedding, the raindrops are only tears the bride won't have to shed later." As the newlywed couple strolled out of the chapel to their home, they came face-to-face with two armed German guards in battle-stained uniforms. But the guards only smiled and congratulated them on their marriage.

As a young girl, my mother had prayed for three things: never to marry a farmer, never to have a red-headed child, and never to be a nun. The first of her prayers had not been granted, and nine months later another one was denied. At the beginning of the summer of 1941, I was born, and she had a red-haired son of a farmer. But she loved us both, and—as far as I know—she has not become a nun yet.

The sounds of war echoed throughout the early years of my childhood. We knew that the Americans had entered the war, but our first contact with them was as a noise rumbling across the sky like thunder. My mother was giving my younger brother Gérard and me a bath outdoors on a warm morning when American and British warplanes—which were supposed to be coming to our rescue—suddenly banked out of the clouds and strafed the earthen berms beside the milk house. With a wet, naked child under each arm she dashed to my father, who was calmly sitting on a tractor, plowing his field. The tractor was so loud that he couldn't hear a thing and didn't notice that all around him the workers were running wildly for

cover. Luckily, the planes didn't seem to consider his tractor a military target. My parents could not understand why the Allies were firing on farms, but they later learned that the pilots had mistaken the berms for German tanks.

August 15th, the Feast of the Virgin Mary, is always a special day in France, but for us in 1945, we gave thanks even more than usual. Though I was only four, I will never forget that day. We were on our way to church in our horse-drawn carriage, wearing our white gloves as always, when some trucks came lumbering down the road at us. Gérard and I could sense that something unforgettable was happening. The trucks were filled with American soldiers, smiling and waving, and our little hands waved back like excited white butterflies. These gentle warriors with dirty faces and warm smiles stopped long enough to give my parents cigarettes and some gasoline for our automobile. I thought they were the most beautiful faces I had ever seen, and my mother is certain that then and there I made up my mind to say "Merci, America" in person.

A COUNTRY CHILDHOOD

France was free, peace descended on the valley, and Gérard and I also discovered freedom. We ran with our dog through the fields, leaving the milk house at dawn and not returning until long after daylight had departed the meadows. There was no better place to spend an afternoon than in a cherry tree, spitting the pits as far as we could while we devoured the cherries. We were never separated, and Maman accused of us being each other's shadow. We were fourteen months apart in age, and only once was there a hint of jealousy. When I caught whooping cough, Gérard was mad because he did not get it too.

We knew every inch of the woods, caves, the farms, and the houses, even the underground passage that led from the château to an old monastery for women two miles away. We always took our pet goat, Biquette, to celebrate Mass at the chapel. She sat between Gérard and me very politely and never joined in the singing—unless, of course, it was a song she really liked.

What we liked most in those days was to have lunch with the farmers in their houses. Gérard and I would sneak out and eat with them whenever we could. They were always generous and good, and we became part of their family. Farmers did not exactly live in the Middle Ages, but they did keep some very old ways. Everyone had his or her own plate, knife, fork, spoon, and mug. The plate was very deep, and the soup, then the meat and the vegetable, were all served on it, using bread to clean it between courses. At the end of the meal, a farmer would once again clean the plate with bread, turn it over, and eat his cheese and dessert off the bottom. Everyone took care of their own plate, cleaning it and putting it away in a box after the meal. When you only have one plate and you get hungry three times a day, you make sure nothing happens to it.

Lunch with the farmers was a regular part of our carefree life, but other things we did were a little more irregular. We generally went ahead and did them anyway, but we did not share those things with our parents until we were quite sure that the statute of limitations had run out—at least two decades later. Perhaps that was why Maman always said that in childhood you really build your heaven or your hell. There were egg fights that left our best clothes dripping with yolk, shells, and mud. We would steal away with our parents' car, even before our feet could reach the pedals. And there was hide-and-seek with our little cousins, up in the hay,

where we were not supposed to be. Madame Henriette, our nanny for three generations, was our co-conspirator in keeping these secrets. Regardless of the mischief we made, Madame Henriette stood behind us and did everything she could to hide our shenanigans from our parents. Maybe that was what taught me that liberty is something you keep only if you give it to others.

Her real genius, however, was in the kitchen, and at our meals I learned the true essence of French country cooking. Even at an early age, I found myself helping to choose the daily menu. It was a game we played first thing in the morning. Madame Henriette would ask "Now, Patrick, what shall we plan for the menu today?"

I would say, "Today, we should have green peas and tomatoes," if that was what I was hungry for. Then she would go to Maman and say, "Madame, you know the green peas are really good this time of year" and "I saw the tomatoes early this morning, and they have never been bigger or juicier." This was my first lesson in the art of negotiation—make the other person want what you want.

"Very good," Maman would answer. "Then let's have green peas and tomatoes for lunch."

André, the gardener, would harvest all the vegetables by ten o'clock, according to Madame Henriette's order. They would be on our plates by half past noon, along with fresh flowers on the table. I would look over the table and believe in my little heart that I was actually responsible for the family's meal each day. I was very proud and happy.

Of course there was always an appetizer, a main course, a vegetable, a salad, cheese, fruit, and wine for the adults and cider for the children. All prepared with the genius of Madame Henriette's and Maman's recipes. I did not realize until many years later that my ideas for lunch and dinner were actually Madame Henriette's. She just smiled and let me take the credit.

Madame Henriette was my teacher, my confidante, and my best friend. Her mother, Berthe, had already been at the château when she came to work there at the age of eighteen. Madame Henriette had been raised on a farm and was blessed with more common sense than anyone I have ever known. Her claim to greatness, however, was her genuine flair for cooking. She baked cookies called "tuiles" that attracted the greedy hands of two little brothers until she chased us out of the kitchen, shaking her apron at us as though she were shooing flies away. She also created wonderful apricot, blackberry, and rhubarb preserves. When I go back to France now, the first thing I ask for is one of her apple tarts. Nobody bakes them quite like she does, and they still taste as good as my memory says they should.

Every meal was a ceremony, a time for the family to be together. And it was a celebration, as we learned to entertain ourselves with conversation. We children were invited to participate as much as anyone, and we all felt free to express our opinions and our ideas, no matter how ridiculous they might seem. We went to school like everyone else, but our real education was around the dining table.

At the head of the table, my father didn't talk much, but when he did, he had something to say. He was like a gardener. He gave us directions and the freedom to be ourselves, to think for ourselves, and the confidence to lead our own lives. He was a good man, tender and decisive, humble but tenacious. When he wanted something he got it. When he decided to do something he did it. His friends called him "l'Intouchable," meaning that he was irreproachable.

My mother demanded the best from herself and from others. She was very giving, and she gave us strength. Her zest for life constantly created new experiences for us and challenged us to do the best we could. She always wanted things done the right way, especially in the kitchen and on the table. She created good things in her life, especially her love, to share with others.

Gérard and I were the wanderers, our younger sister, Joëlle, was the tomboy, and Franck was the unexpected one, the afterthought. One day fourteen years after Joëlle was born (nineteen after I was born), my father told my mother, as tenderly as he knew how, that he wanted another child.

My mother was adamant; she had no desire to have a baby at the age of forty. But, as I said, my father was tenacious. When my mother found out she was pregnant, she smiled at François and said softly, "You caught me by surprise." Some months later, Franck was born.

Their love has been like the bloom on a rare, magical rose, one that does not fade with the passing years. When I was seventeen, my grandmother left Château les Pins for Paris, leaving the white limestone building for our family. But as beautiful as the château was, my mother did not want to leave the milk house. She had been a bride there; she had raised her children there.

Madame Henriette took Maman on a grand tour of the château, trying to convince her of the convenience and beauty of her new home. "Madame will see how much happier she will be here," Madame Henriette said. "When you stand on the terrace, the sun is everywhere. The air up here is as pure as the country itself." Maman was impressed, but she still looked wistfully down at the milk house, and for days she cried every time she saw it.

We had many good years in the château, but time promises nothing. My father worked hard to make the thousand-acre farm at les Pins a success, but the economy was bad. Prices plummeted, and the franc dried up. My father had too much pride to declare bankruptcy, and he was forced to sell the land and the château that had been part of the family for so long.

Both in their fifties, my parents walked away from the earth that held their roots so deeply. My mother and father were forced to start all over again. After having had their own gardeners and maids, my father, as dignified as ever, became the head gardener at a large estate and my mother accepted a job caring for other people's children. But they had each other, their love, and their love for their children. Perhaps that was all they ever wanted or needed; certainly it was enough to see them through. Adversity only strengthened them, as it strengthened us children and the whole family. I learned from them that no matter what you are doing, you have to do it well, and with your head held high.

MAKING AN IDEA WORK

The years passed, I began my career in Paris, and everything seemed to be going my way. I had my own marketing company. I lived and worked on a mahogany yacht built for the Vanderbilts in 1905 and now docked in the shadow of the Eiffel Tower. My life was so happy I never considered moving. But sometimes I would watch the ducks fly past the Pont d'Alma and I would admire their lives. They flew so fast and so high; they were cute, humble, and fun. If it rained or froze, they could fly off to Africa—and do it with a light-hearted "quack."

Then in 1979, I received a telephone call from an American friend, Sue de Brantes, who had married Marquis Paul de Brantes and become a marquise. "I've met an oil and gas man from Oklahoma who wants to do business with you," she said. Mr. Oil and Gas Man first said he wanted to organize big rodeos to travel throughout Europe, but I told him there had not been a successful rodeo in Europe since Buffalo Bill brought over his Wild West Show. Besides, in Europe, we don't ride steaks, we eat them. The next year, he wanted to capitalize on the craze for John Travolta and *Urban Cowboy*, but I told him in Europe it was just a fad that would ride off into the sunset pretty quickly.

He didn't give up easily, however; he was determined to bring the west to Europe. I thought perhaps we should go the other direction. On one of his trips, I had taken him to visit Raoul, my old friend who had a vineyard where he served wine, bread, sausage, and cheese. His hospitality was so good that both he and his vineyard became legendary. Raoul's family had lived there for generations, and the walls of his cellar were lined with bottles and barrels of wine. In 1870, Raoul's grandfather had seen the clouds of war between France and Germany gathering, and he buried all his wine in the sandy soil of his cellar. Raoul is still finding vintages from before 1870 buried in the sand of his cellar.

When I went to Raoul's with Mr. Oil and Gas Man, the wine was so good and the bread so fresh and fragrant that I suggested we build an authentic French bakery in America, one modeled on Raoul's old limestone cellar. I had the strange feeling that the Southwest needed good French bread a lot more than Europe needed rodeos, bucking bulls, or honky-tonks!

"Do you cook?" his banker wanted to know.

"I know what good food is," I explained. That seemed to be good enough for him—perhaps it was my English, which was freely mixed with French phrases and accented by a lot of frantic and hopeful gestures. Mr. Oil and Gas Man thought I should start in Dallas, though I barely knew where Dallas was on the map.

A few days after I arrived in Dallas, the manager of a gourmet store listened to my idea and said, "I'm meeting with Stanley Marcus. Why don't you come along?" I shall be forever grateful to Susie Rothstein, but at the time I said, "Who is Stanley Marcus?" I knew nothing of Mr. Marcus or his fabulous stores.

Susie only laughed.

When we met, Mr. Marcus asked what I was doing in Dallas. "I'm here to open a French bakery," I answered. I saw a spark of interest in his eyes. "If it is an authentic French country bakery, and if you put it near Southern Methodist University," he said, "it will be a success." That turned out to be the best piece of advice I received. I didn't know any more about SMU than I did about Dallas or Stanley Marcus, but I found an empty store in a small shopping center across the street from the SMU football field.

The landlord could barely understand my broken English. He asked for a guaranty, but I had nothing in America. He asked what my assets were. I wasn't sure what the word "assets" meant, and my trusty pocket French-English dictionary was no help. "Anything with exchange value," it said.

I have the feeling the landlord was not impressed with my response. Finally he said, "Okay, here's the deal. The rent's twenty dollars a square foot with no allowance for improvements.

You have a three-year lease and you owe the first year's rent in advance."

I nearly fainted. "I can't afford this," I sighed, "which is a terrible shame, because Mr. Marcus said I should definitely put my bakery near SMU."

The landlord looked up quickly and asked, "Do you know Mr. Marcus?"

I suddenly realized that Mr. Marcus's name had magic—perhaps he should have been the definition of "asset" in my dictionary. I said, "Yes, of course. May I use your phone?" Luckily, Mr. Marcus was at his desk, and I explained the deal I'd been offered. He asked to speak to the landlord.

After they spoke, the landlord turned to me and said, "After reflecting on the situation, I've decided to charge you fourteen dollars a square foot, put in $50,000 in improvements, and give you a nine-year lease. Oh, and I'll only need a month's rent in advance."

I began to understand who Stanley Marcus was.

With the help of Mr. Oil and Gas Man's banker, I thought I was all set. But then he would schedule meetings and cancel them; my phone calls went unanswered and unreturned. Then I saw the headlines: Penn Square Bank was bankrupt, and so was Mr. Oil and Gas Man's banker. And so, I feared, was I.

It seemed that no one in Dallas was willing to invest in a bakery to be started from nothing by someone who was not a baker, not a restaurateur, not a banker, not wealthy, and perhaps worst of all, not even a Texan. I heard many different kinds of excuses from potential investors, many of which were undoubtedly true. They were sorry. I was broke, a word that I learned in America.

Finally, one of my best friends back in France agreed to help me. Bernard didn't know if Texas was hungry for a loaf of French bread, but he believed in me and my ideas. He gave me enough money to pursue the project, and we shook hands, which was as satisfactory to him as a bunch of legal papers. Bernard is now a happy man.

CREATING A FRENCH BAKERY

My favorite pastime was to sit on the sidewalk in front of the gaping, empty corner of a shopping center that was my future bakery. People would walk by, stare at the hole, and then ask in their friendly Texas way, "What's going to be there?"

"A French bakery," I'd reply.

"Is it going to have a hearthstone oven?"

I'd scribble in my notebook, "Put in a hearthstone oven."

Someone else asked, "Are you going to have wooden beams?"

"Wooden beams" would go in the notebook.

My future guests became the architects of the bakery, and they wanted a rustic country French atmosphere. The hearthstone oven became my wood-burning one. Stacks of wood were piled in the bakery, and there was just the right weathering on the antique bricks and wooden beams. They wanted antiques from France and baker's tools in the dining room, along with chairs of woven straw. And there were fresh flowers, to remind me of those meals around the dining table of my boyhood home. For the antique beams, I even brought a carpenter from a village near where I was born. It was the first time he had ever left the area around his home. But he was a craftsman who understood France and the French country atmosphere I was determined to re-create in the bakery.

I wanted the facade fashioned with brick, wood, and glass, but the landlord wanted me to use stucco, like the other businesses in the center. I took a risk. "I will put the bricks on the facade myself, but if I get one single complaint, I will take them out and replace them with stucco at my own expense." No one has ever complained.

My bakery was beginning to have a shape, but it didn't have a name yet. I wanted a name that would be easy for Americans to pronounce and remember. It had to be a recognizably French name, preferably one that evoked Paris, and one that was linked to food. And, of course, there should be a story behind it.

I used my system for solving a problem. I thought about it all day, I wrote it on my bedroom mirror, and I went to sleep. My mind worked all night, and when I awoke that summer morning, the answer was waiting for me.

La Madeleine is the name of a church in Paris named for Mary Magdalene. It is said that Napoléon ordered it to be built in an area infamous for its ladies of the night, because a church would be the best way to cleanse the neighborhood and give it a better reputation. Now, generations later, there may be a few who still walk the street, but there are also fine restaurants like Lucas Carton, little cafés, tearooms like Ladurée, pastry shops, and gourmet stores like Fauchon's that serve the best food and wines.

And of course, French novelist Marcel Proust wrote about the little cakes that are called madeleines. Finally, there is the beloved story about a little girl in Paris named Madeline. She was small, but her heart was big, and everyone loved her.

La Madeleine, I decided, was the perfect name.

All that remained now was for la Madeleine to bake its first loaf of French bread. André, whose family had been bakers for generations, came to Dallas to re-create the kind of bread I had when I was a child. During my childhood in the Loire Valley, during those war years, our family grew and prepared everything for the table except bread. The baker in the village had a car powered by a wood-burning engine, and his wife delivered the bread to the farms every week. We could hear the old car sputtering through the valley long after the sun had fallen beyond the hills. Finally, always late, some time around ten o'clock, the baker's wife would arrive with the bread. We called her Mrs. Moonlight. The bread was just a simple mixture of flour, water, leaven, very little or no yeast, and a pinch of salt. It was pure and healthy, and a meal was not a meal without it.

At la Madeleine, we would bake our bread fresh every day, using the same ingredients: flour, water, leaven, all-natural yeast or no yeast, and a pinch of salt. It is a recipe that has been handed down in Europe for centuries, and there are no shortcuts. It takes our bakers 6 hours to make the bread, carefully shaping it by hand and baking it in the wood-fired oven. It is a simple formula, high in fiber, without cholesterol or fat, and it works pretty well.

To bake the bread the authentic, old-fashioned way causes the fermenting leaven to create little pockets of air, little holes, in the dough. In France, we can always tell how good a loaf really is by the number of holes in a slice. That is French; that is tradition.

On the first day the bakery was open, we sold maybe five hundred loaves of bread. That was good, I thought, but not all my customers did. Many came back saying, "We can't make sandwiches with your bread. Everything falls through the holes!" Americans wanted sandwiches, and America was my new country. So overnight we adjusted the recipe to create the best bread we could with the smallest holes we could.

My first guests also helped by demanding soups, salads, and sandwiches in addition to the breads and pastries we were serving. I smiled reassuringly, but inside I was feeling something more like panic. Nothing I knew how to make would be the same quality as our baked goods. So I did what I thought any professional would do; I picked up the telephone and called an expert. "Maman," I said, "take the next flight to Dallas. We need to learn how to make soups, salads, and sandwiches the way you make them at home."

Maman arrived in our kitchen looking as though she were dressed for a party. Instead she was introduced to big ovens, big mixing bowls, big bakers, and big bags of flour. She promptly rolled up her designer silk sleeves, put on an apron and baker's hat, and set to work. She said she felt like she was in the middle of a perpetual waltz, spinning and whirling from the ovens to the bins to the mixers without a stop, smiling and encouraging us with "Bon . . . Bon." She had no English, but she did have her own French country recipes, and she added what la Madeleine had been missing. Her soups, salads, and quiches flew out the door; we had no leftovers.

One morning Maman came running to me saying that she had been helping one of our cooks, Maria, who had created a wonderful dressing for Caesar salad. No, no, no, I said. Caesar salad is not French. La Madeleine would never serve a Caesar salad. It was out of the question.

You do not say things like that to my mother.

I returned from a business trip to discover that la Madeleine was serving a Caesar salad. Not only that, but everyone said that the Caesar salad, with its special la Madeleine dressing, was the best they had ever eaten. I listened. I have discovered that the secret of business is to listen. Finally I came to a decision. The salad certainly did not come from France, but it should have.

Our Caesar Salad has become a la Madeleine tradition, so popular that I knew we had to serve it, and to serve it exactly as my mother and Maria had created it. When my mother returned home, I asked Maria to give me the recipe. "There is no recipe," Maria said. "Your mother and I simply put this and that together, and I try to keep doing it the same way every day."

I felt an old friend, panic. As calmly as possible, I told her, "Let's put the recipe on paper together." But with me looking over her shoulder, Maria became nervous. She couldn't remember how much of which ingredients should go into the recipe. Finally I left her alone, and she had no trouble at all making the dressing. What could I do? I left her alone to prepare the dressing, and then I spied on her, scribbling down notes whenever she wasn't looking. At last I had the whole recipe on paper, and I promptly locked it away. That recipe has become la Madeleine's greatest treasure.

From the beginning, our number-one priority has been to serve all-natural, homemade, fresh and tasty dishes. After my mother got us started, Rémy Schaal, our head chef, along with his team of bakers and chefs, has continued this tradition, developing new recipes to tempt our guests, and I am very grateful to them for this.

Julia Child once wrote, "Often there are no meals at home and there's no family gathering place. Eating at the dinner table is important; it emphasizes the pleasure of a family getting together." Julia Child made me realize that most people live a "box life." The biggest box is a house. Inside that box is another box called the refrigerator. Inside that box are the ham, cheese, and bread, already sliced, all in the shape of a box. Then we put all these ingredients together inside another box, one that we call a sandwich.

Then we sit on furniture that looks like a box, in front of a box called the television. It talks but does not listen. We sleep on a box, then wake up the next morning and drive to work in a box.

La Madeleine is designed to be a place where our guests can get out of their boxes, where the pleasure of a family eating together can be enjoyed as I did in my childhood in France. At la Madeleine, our guests can say to themselves, "I am living my own life. I can sit here peacefully and read my book, or I can talk to others. I can create. I can share my thoughts with someone else, and they can share their thoughts with me." That is our intent at la Madeleine, and we hope that is the way you will feel if you have a chance to try it for yourself.

INTRODUCTION TO FRENCH COUNTRY COOKING

Is America really ready for another French cookbook?

Yes. And here's why.

Traditionally in this country, French cooking has meant difficult techniques, complicated recipes, and exotic, expensive equipment and ingredients. It represented the kind of special-occasion fare found in fine restaurants rather than at home.

Lately, however, travel and the availability of fresh products from around the world have heightened America's appreciation for regional differences in the food and life of France. Family-style bistros and cafés have encouraged home cooks worldwide to explore their more casual charms.

What has been lacking is a hands-on cookbook compiled by native French cooks preparing simple, healthy, everyday meals for family and guests alike. One of the finest is my mother, Monique Esquerré. She has always looked upon a meal as an experience that—simple or elegant—proclaims the continuing tradition of excellence in French cooking. In this cookbook she introduces her French country recipes to American kitchens.

Married since 1940, the mother of four, a successful cookbook author in France, she began married life in the fabled Touraine, a province long favored by French nobles who built such great country manors that the area is known as "The Château Country." This beautiful region in the Loire Valley—where the purest French is spoken—is also referred to as the Garden of France. Justly famed for its fine wines, goat cheeses, and mushrooms, it was the place chosen by the kings of France for their favorite pastime, hunting.

Breathtaking châteaux were built there from the early Renaissance until the middle of the nineteenth century. Les Pins was one of those châteaux and, more important to me, our home for many years. We were the very fortunate recipients of all the beautiful fruits and vegetables that wonderfully rich soil had to offer. Since les Pins was a working farm, we were always provided with the freshest seasonal produce, meats, and dairy products.

My family's lifestyle changed to some extent in the 1970s when my mother and father moved near Paris. It was a much simpler life for my mother than during the days she served as mistress of les Pins. One thing remained the same, however: those wonderful smells wafting from the kitchen. Mother's culinary creations were always a labor of love.

Her first cookbook, written as part of an award-winning series in France, shared her sound expertise, but only in France. In 1983 I had the opportunity to introduce her cooking to America at la Madeleine. I have always believed that the finest compliment a cook can receive is for guests to ask for a recipe. La Madeleine patrons, delighted by the dishes my mother developed, are always demanding her recipes.

Now, for the first time in America, we can reveal her prime secrets: simplicity, healthy dishes, the use of the finest products, along with the extra tender loving care she gives each recipe.

The style of cooking is based on good common sense and nature. It's a varied diet of good food that is also good for your health, what we call in France "le bon et le bien." Food that is fresh, wholesome, and tastes good is also healthy food.

The problem occurs when there is no variety or balance in the diet. We use a lot of herbs, virgin olive oil, and basic healthy ingredients, balanced, of course, with the traditional method of French country cooking, taking advantage of the flavor of butter and cream when they add something special to a recipe.

In a reader-friendly format this cookbook will guide even the beginning cook in the art of contemporary French country cooking: dishes simple enough for everyday family meals, yet created with a flair sufficient for important dinner guests. Many of the recipes and cooking tips have been passed down through generations of farmers. Others have been adapted from friends whose recipes we find very interesting and like very much. We have signed their names to the recipes they so generously contributed to the cookbook. Otherwise, the recipes come from the Esquerré family.

What I have attempted to do in this cookbook is share the simplicity, the quality, the taste, the ways of life from my old country with my new one. All of the recipes are reasonably simple and involve ingredients readily available in American supermarkets. There is also a glossary of French cooking terms and their explanations.

We have included a collection of Reci Tips and French Maxims that give you hints on preparing the ingredients, as well as a better understanding of the French way of life, the roots of French country cooking and the French appreciation for good food. Recipes that are especially easy are marked with a "Très Simple" at the top of the page. They are designed for the cook who has little or no experience, or for more seasoned cooks looking for time-saving recipes. I have also included a guide to French wines, one that I believe can help you find a harmony between good foods and good wines. And I have provided a list of my favorite restaurants and bistros in the regions of France I am most familiar with: the Loire, Burgundy, and the Château Country. The atmosphere is always warm and hospitable, and the food is wonderful.

These are basic, tasty recipes, but you can be as creative, as inventive, as you want. In France there is a constant contest among everyone who cooks, a constant challenge to take a good recipe and make it better. Cooking is the national sport of France. And it seems to be a very healthy sport.

Dr. Joe D. Goldstrich, a board-certified cardiologist specializing in preventive and nutritional cardiology, recently wrote: "For as long as I can remember, the French have been renowned for their fine dining. Only recently have we come to realize that despite their passion for food, drink, and the other pleasures of life, they suffer a much lower rate of cardiovascular disease than Americans. Recent medical research has shed some light on this apparent 'French paradox.'

"The liberal use of olive oil, vegetables, garlic, onions, herbs, seafood, pasta, fruits and red wine all play an important role in this 'Mediterranean diet.' You can always count on authentic French recipes to blend good taste with healthful eating."

So is America ready for another book on French cooking?

Now you be the judge.

—Patrick Esquerré

INGREDIENTS FOR BECOMING A GOOD COOK

The success of any recipe lies in four basic things.

1. Begin with the freshest and the best ingredients possible. This greatly enhances the final taste. Train yourself to seek recipes that best fit the season. This simply means you make a winter soup like Potage Paysan during the winter months, and serve asparagus in the spring. The ingredients you select will be fresh, have a good color, a fragrant aroma, and real flavor.

2. Organization and preparation play a big role in the outcome of your recipe. The French term "mise en place" means everything in its place. Translated to cooking, this means you will have read the recipe thoroughly and properly prepared each ingredient before you begin cooking. I suggest using a tray to help organize the ingredients. Chop the vegetables, measure them, and set them on the tray. Do this with each ingredient so there are no surprises in the middle of preparation. If you have measured your dairy products or meat you must return them to the refrigerator if they are not used at the beginning of the recipe. Set out any utensils or equipment you may need along the way. This "mise en place" will help produce a successful recipe by reducing error and putting you at ease during the actual cooking. Be neat and clean in your preparation. Do dishes as you go along so the end of your meal is not spent toiling in the kitchen all night.

3. Dust off your common sense and use it for cooking. If the recipe calls for an ingredient or a pan you do not have, a substitute will do as well. Many herbs can be interchanged. This might alter the flavor of the dish somewhat, but that is all right if you like the taste. If sometimes a recipe is very different, yet the dish is good and edible, simply rename it. You may be the only one who knows or cares.

Often people tend to use shortcuts, losing the basic ingredients of what gives mankind a sense of the good life, a touch of European tenderness, as well as flavors from the Old World. For example, bread can be made in two hours, but it takes several hours to make good bread. To some, it may seem that baking takes too much time. But the taste of good bread is always worth the extra time.

4. Think about your food when you bring it to the table. Remember, people eat with their eyes first. A sprig of parsley, basil, rosemary, or sage might be just the thing to decorate your platter. Think about colors when selecting your menu. A bright combination of colors is much more appealing than a dish where everything has pretty much the same coloration. You might also consider decorating the table with fresh flowers in the summer and holly in the winter. Your family and guests will appreciate the extra touch. Each recipe has its own personality and you should do your best to reveal it to those who dine with you. Sharing at the table is an essential ingredient for friendship.

Above all, relax and have fun cooking.

Be creative.

Be inventive.

If a recipe doesn't work, try it again. You will be glad you did.

—Monique Esquerré

MENU SUGGESTIONS

WINTER

Lunches

Small Hot Ham Turnovers (p. 55),
Salmon in Parchment (p. 85), Potatoes au Gratin (p. 103),
Easy Chocolate Cake (p. 112) with English Cream (p. 128)

Winter Salad (p. 46),
Beef in Shallot Sauce (p. 75), White Onion Purée (p. 100),
Almond Lace Cookies (p. 115)

Salmon Rillettes (p. 61),
Spinach and Sausage Bread (pp. 39–40), Composed Salad (p.136),
Pears Poached in Red Wine (p. 124)

Dinners

Gruyère Cheese Straws (p. 59),
Pot-au-Feu (p. 76), steamed potatoes, Pepper Salad (p. 45),
Madame Henriette's Tart (p. 120)

Peasant-Style Soup (p. 35),
Stuffed Family-Style Veal Scallop (p. 71), Buttered Endives (p. 97),
Aunt Lucie's Tart (p. 120)

SPRING

Lunches

Marbled Eggs (p. 58), Lamb Stew with Fresh Spring Vegetables (p. 79),
Coupe Martinique (p. 141) with Madeleine Cakes (p. 111)

Grand Duchess Salad (p. 50),
Chicken with Lemons (p. 68), Quick Endives (p. 139),
Emperor's Omelette with Compote of Plums (p. 121)

Dinners

Marinated Yellow and Red Peppers (p. 135) on lettuce
with lemon and sliced baguette,
Filet of Sole and Salmon Braised in Cream (p. 86), Parisian Potatoes (p. 104),
Lemon Soufflé (p. 122)

Red Bell Pepper Bavarois (p. 60) with mixed spring lettuce and Vinaigrette (pp. 51–52),
Trout with Chives (p. 84), White Onion Purée (p. 100),
Almond Tartlets with Fruit Preserves (p. 116)

SUMMER

Lunches

Salad from Southern France (p. 44),
Chicken Salad with Almonds (p. 49), Bread from Nice (p. 38),
Raspberry Tart (p. 117)

Pepper Salad (p. 45),
Scallops on a Skewer with Olive-Anchovy Sauce (p. 87), French Pasta (p. 105),
Melon Surprise (p. 141)

Dinners

Radish Canapés (p. 136),
Gazpacho in a Jiffy (p. 36), Ham Terrine (p. 56), Tarragon Chicken (p. 65),
Fruit Sherbet (p. 125) with Fresh Fruit Sauce (p. 126)

Chilled Cucumber Soup (p. 33),
Braised Beef (p. 77), Stuffed Potatoes (p. 139),
Almond Lace Cookies (p. 115) with whipped cream and fresh fruit

FALL

Lunches

la Madeleine Caesar Salad (p. 47),
Cassoulet (pp. 80–81), Ratatouille (p. 101),
Quick Apple Tart (p. 119)

Hot Duck Salad Château de la Marchère (p. 43),
Peasant-Style Soup (p. 35),
Assorted Breads with Strawberry Preserves (p. 143),
Petit Fours Glacés (p. 142)

Dinners

Carrot Soup with Tomatoes (p. 32),
Quail with Red Bell Peppers (p. 69),
Potatoes au Gratin (p. 103), Grenadine Onion Preserves (p. 96),
Apple Cake (p. 110)

Onion Soup (p. 34), Pheasant in a Pot (p. 70),
Parisian Potatoes (p. 104), Provençal Tomatoes (p. 102),
Pear Tart (p. 118)

ELABORATE DINNERS

Oysters in a Bowl (p. 83), Winter Salad (p. 46),
Champagne Chicken (p. 66), Carrot Purée (p. 99),
Chocolate Marquise Royale (p. 114) with Raspberry Sauce (p. 109) and/or English Cream (p. 128)

Aperitif, Gruyère Cheese Straws (p. 59), Zucchini Salad with Mushrooms (p. 48),
Pork Roast with Oranges (p. 78), Vegetable Terrine (p. 57),
Hazelnut Cake with Raspberry Sauce (p. 109)

ZERO-FAT MEALS

Half melon; tomatoes, mushrooms, peppers, garlic,
and parsley cooked in reduced herbed wine,
Lettuce Salad with Vinaigrette Zero (p. 52), baguette,
Fruit Sherbet (p. 125) with Fresh Fruit Sauce (p. 126)

Red Bell Pepper Bavarois (p. 60) on baguette,
Jean-Luc's Pot-au-Feu de Légumes (p. 140),
Pears Poached in Red Wine (p. 124)

SOUPS AND BREADS

Brie Soup
Soupe au Brie

Carrot Soup with Tomatoes
Soupe de Carottes à la Tomates

Chilled Cucumber Soup
Soupe Glacée au Concombre

Onion Soup
Soupe à l'Oignon Gratinée

Peasant-Style Soup
Potage Paysan

Gazpacho in a Jiffy
Gazpacho Express

Country Bread with Apples
Pain Campagnard aux Pommes

Bread from Nice
Pain de Nice

Spinach and Sausage Bread
Pain aux Epinards et à la Saucisse

Brie Soup
Soupe au Brie

Très Simple

Preparation: 10 minutes
Cooking: 25 minutes
Servings: 4
Equipment: 2½-quart saucepan,
whisk, 8-inch skillet

INGREDIENTS

2 tablespoons unsalted butter
1 large onion, peeled and
chopped (about 1 cup)
1 rib celery, chopped
2 tablespoons flour
3 cups chicken or vegetable stock
(or 2 chicken bouillon cubes
dissolved in 3 cups water)
1 cup milk
½ pound Brie or Camembert
cheese, rind removed
¼ pound fresh cream cheese or
puréed cottage cheese
Salt to taste
Freshly ground pepper to taste
Parsley for garnish

INGREDIENTS

4 slices firm white bread, crusts
removed
2 tablespoons unsalted butter
2 tablespoons minced parsley

Yield: 1 quart

Brie Soup is particularly good when the weather turns cool. It is a creamy, luscious soup that can become the first course for a party, or, with Hot Duck Salad (p. 43), a quick supper beside the fire. For those who appreciate a stronger flavor, try using Camembert, another soft-ripened cheese.

Melt butter in a large saucepan and cook onion and celery over low heat for 5 minutes. Add flour and whisk until combined. Slowly add stock and milk, whisking to prevent lumps. Simmer for 15 minutes, uncovered.

Cut cheese into small pieces. Blend cheese into the liquid along with cream cheese, stirring until just melted. Season soup with salt and pepper. Serve hot with croutons on top and garnish with chopped fresh parsley.

Croutons

Cut bread into desired shape (triangle, circle, heart, square). Melt butter in small skillet and sauté bread until golden brown. Dip croutons into parsley and place on top of soup.

Reci Tip—To keep cheese fresh, store with a sugar lump in a
cheese box.
—Danielle Renard

Carrot Soup with Tomatoes
Soupe de Carottes à la Tomates

Preparation: 30 minutes
Cooking: 40 minutes
Servings: 6
Equipment: 6-quart ovenproof baking dish, blender, small bowl

INGREDIENTS

2 tablespoons unsalted butter
2 medium onions, peeled and cut in rings
1 pound carrots, peeled and diced
3 tablespoons water
1½ pounds tomatoes (about 5 medium), peeled, seeded, and cut in large pieces
½ teaspoon sugar
2 cloves garlic, peeled and crushed
1 sprig thyme
4½ cups chicken stock (or substitute 4 chicken bouillon cubes dissolved in 4½ cups water)
Salt to taste
Freshly ground pepper to taste
¾ cup heavy cream
2 egg yolks
Chervil or thyme for garnish

Carrots and tomatoes give this soup a beautiful color. Different and delicious, the soup is equally good without the cream and egg yolks. If you leave them out, however, thin the soup with additional stock or water.

Melt butter in large saucepan, add onions and carrots, and cook over medium heat 5 minutes. Add water. Simmer for 15 minutes, covered, until carrots are tender.

Add tomatoes, sugar, garlic, thyme, stock, and bring gently to a boil. Turn down heat and simmer for 15 minutes, covered.

Allow mixture to cool briefly, then purée in a blender.

Pour soup into a clean saucepan and simmer for 5 minutes. Season with salt and pepper. Remove from heat.

Whip cream with egg yolks in a small bowl. Stir some of the hot mixture into the bowl to temper the eggs; gently blend this mixture back into the soup. Stir well; do not boil or mixture will separate. Check seasoning. Garnish with chopped fresh chervil or thyme sprigs.

—la Madeleine

Reci Tip—When choosing fresh carrots, select those with the greenest leaves.

Chilled Cucumber Soup
Soupe Glacée au Concombre

Très Simple

Preparation: 20 minutes, plus 3
  hours refrigeration
Cooking: 45 minutes
Servings: 6
Equipment: 6-quart saucepan,
  blender, whisk

INGREDIENTS

1 large cucumber, seeded,
  peeled, and coarsely chopped
  (set aside ¼ cup for use as
  decoration)
1 large onion, peeled and
  chopped (about 1 cup)
3 cups milk
3 cups chicken stock (or substitute 3 chicken bouillon cubes
  dissolved in 3 cups water)
Salt to taste
Freshly ground pepper to taste
2 tablespoons unsalted butter
¼ cup flour
1 tablespoon chopped fresh mint
¾ cup heavy cream or low-fat
  sour cream

This is my brother Franck's recipe. Franck is 20 years my junior, and we call him "afterthought" because his birth was such a surprise. We really should rename this "afterthought soup," as it's one of Franck's favorite recipes. Franck is one of those wonderful cooks who needs to prepare at least one meal a day to feel right about himself.
—*Patrick Esquerré*

Place all but ¼ cup of the cucumber in a large saucepan with chopped onion, milk, stock, salt, and pepper. Simmer slowly for 30 minutes, uncovered. Set mixture aside to cool slightly. Transfer contents to a blender and purée, in 2 batches if necessary.

Melt butter in a clean pan, add flour, and stir for 2–3 minutes with whisk. Remove pan from heat and add puréed mixture, a little at a time, whisking constantly.

Return pan to medium heat and stir for 5–6 minutes. Stir in mint. Pour into a soup tureen, cover with clear plastic film to prevent a skin from forming, and chill in the refrigerator for 3 hours.

Sprinkle remaining cucumber with a pinch of salt and refrigerate.

Just before serving, whip cream into the soup. Blot the diced cucumber and use it to garnish soup.
—*Franck Esquerré*

French Maxim—The discovery of a new dish creates more happiness for the human race than the discovery of a new star.

Onion Soup
Soupe à l'Oignon Gratinée

Preparation: 20 minutes
Cooking: 1 hour
Servings: 4
Equipment: 2½-quart heavy
    saucepan, ovenproof bowls,
    baking sheet

INGREDIENTS

1 tablespoon extra virgin olive oil
2 medium onions, peeled and
    thinly sliced
1 bay leaf
¼ tablespoon freshly ground
    pepper
2 cloves garlic, chopped
½ teaspoon dried thyme
1 quart beef stock (or substitute
    2 cubes bouillon dissolved in 1
    quart water)
4 slices baguette bread, toasted
¾ cup grated Gruyère cheese

This is the onion soup that has become so popular at la Madeleine. It is hearty enough to make a meal in itself, especially when served with bread and Pepper Salad (p. 45), with Pear Tart (p. 118) for dessert. We suggest you make the soup ahead because the flavor improves and mellows.

Heat the olive oil in a large, heavy saucepan. Add onions, bay leaf, and pepper. Sauté over low heat for about 30 minutes, stirring occasionally. The secret to making a great onion soup lies in the slow cooking of the onions. The flavor comes from releasing the sugars in the onions by cooking them until they begin to caramelize. The onions should be a golden brown.

Add garlic and thyme and stir well. Cook for 2 minutes.

Pour beef stock in and bring to a boil, then reduce heat and simmer for 30 minutes, covered.

To serve, ladle soup into individual ovenproof terrines or soup bowls. Place toasted baguette slices on top of the soup and sprinkle with cheese. Place the terrines on a baking sheet under a broiler to melt the cheese and brown the top.   —la Madeleine

Reci Tip—To keep onions fresh longer, pass the roots of the onion across the stove burner. —Friedel Gerber

Peasant-Style Soup
Potage Paysan

Très Simple

Preparation: 20 minutes
Cooking: 40 minutes
Servings: 6
Equipment: 6-quart saucepan or
small stockpot, 8-inch skillet

INGREDIENTS

6 small or 3 large leeks
4 large onions, peeled and
chopped
3 tablespoons extra virgin olive
oil, divided use
1 rib celery, chopped
4 medium potatoes (about 1½
pounds), peeled and sliced
1 bouquet garni (parsley, thyme,
and bay leaf tied together)
1 beef soup bone
8 cups water
Salt to taste
Freshly ground pepper to taste
Thyme, parsley, or chervil for
garnish

In the French countryside, "potage" is the term used for soup.
This Potage Paysan is reminiscent of the traditional dish of
families who till the French farmlands. Together with bread, it
remains even today their basic nourishment. It is a satisfying
and wholesome soup that is high in flavor and low in fat. Serve
with crusty, toasted bread that has been rubbed with the cut
side of a garlic clove.

Trim 2 inches of green parts of leeks and discard. Slice into
⅜-inch rounds, separating green and white parts. Wash thoroughly in a container of water, allowing dirt and sand to fall to
the bottom. Drain leeks and set aside. In a large saucepan over
medium heat, brown onions and green parts of leeks in 2 tablespoons of olive oil. Add celery, potatoes, and bouquet garni. Stir
well and reduce heat to low.

Heat 1 tablespoon of olive oil in a small skillet and cook white
parts of leeks until just browned. Add to the other vegetables
along with the beef bone. Add water to cover vegetables (about
8 cups) and simmer very slowly for 30 minutes.

Remove the bouquet garni. Mash potatoes slightly on the
bottom of the pan and stir well again. Season to taste with salt
and pepper and garnish with thyme, parsley, or chervil.

Gazpacho in a Jiffy
Gazpacho Express

Très Simple

Preparation: 20 minutes, plus
   1 hour refrigeration
Cooking: not required
Servings: 4
Equipment: blender, sharp knife

INGREDIENTS

1 cup cucumber, peeled, seeded,
   and diced
1 cup bell pepper, any color,
   diced
1 cup white onion, diced
2 pounds fully ripe tomatoes
   (about 7 medium), peeled,
   seeded, and quartered
4 tablespoons extra virgin olive
   oil
2 tablespoons red wine vinegar
Salt to taste
Freshly ground pepper to taste
Several basil leaves

The French version of the classic Spanish chilled soup is light, zesty and, above all, healthy. Gazpacho is easy and quick to make, yet subtle and piquant when created with the red, juicy tomatoes of summer. It is the perfect soup to carry along on a picnic, and a sprinkling of la Madeleine's croutons (p. 47) adds an extra crunch that helps Gazpacho make summertime memories.

Sprinkle cucumber with some salt and set aside in a colander for ½ hour to drain. Chill pepper and onion in the refrigerator along with the cucumber, until serving time.

In a blender, purée tomatoes with olive oil and vinegar until smooth. Season with salt and pepper and set aside in refrigerator with some basil leaves immersed in the purée for added flavor. (This amount of tomatoes should yield at least 4 cups of purée.)

Before serving, blot cucumber with a paper towel to remove moisture. Pour gazpacho into cups or soup bowls and garnish with diced pepper, onion, cucumber, and chopped fresh basil.

Serve ice cold.

Reci Tip—When using onions raw, wash them and soak briefly in ice water. Drain them and dry them well. Store in the refrigerator. This brings out the sweetness, eliminates the offensive odor, and crisps them.

Country Bread with Apples
Pain Campagnard aux Pommes

Preparation: 30 minutes, plus
7 hours rising time
Cooking: 40 minutes
Yield: 4 (1¼-pound) loaves
Equipment: mixer, large bowls,
bread pans

INGREDIENTS

3 packages dry yeast, plus 6
tablespoons lukewarm water
(105–115°)
1⅔ cups rye flour (8 ounces)
1⅔ cups whole wheat flour
(8 ounces)
2 cups apple cider
6¾ cups bread or all-purpose
flour (32 ounces)
5 teaspoons salt (1 ounce)
1–2 cups water, as needed to
make dough
2 apples, peeled, cored, diced
(about 3 cups)
Oil or butter for molds

Apples provide just the right flavor to give you the real taste of country cooking. This is an excellent bread, as well as a great breakfast toast. You may think the bread sounds sweet because of the fruit and cider, but it isn't. The apples merely add a subtle flavor. As with all bread, the amount of water needed varies with the flour used and the weather.

Sprinkle dry yeast over 6 tablespoons of lukewarm water. Set aside, in a warm place, for 5 minutes to proof. Mixture will become foamy as the yeast begins to work. Mix yeast together with rye flour, wheat flour, and cider. Set this mixture aside for 6 hours to create a "sponge."

After 6 hours add bread or all-purpose flour, salt, and water (as needed) to the sponge. Start with 1 cup of water and keep adding until a smooth, cohesive dough is achieved. Combine well, then mix in the apples. Knead dough in the mixer at medium speed, using a dough hook if available, for 5 minutes, or by hand for 10 minutes. Place dough in an oiled bowl, cover and let rise 30 minutes, or until doubled in size.

Punch down to expel gases from dough and form into desired loaf shapes. Use standard bread pans or shape into round loaves. Grease bread molds with butter or oil and place dough in the molds to rise for 30 more minutes, or until doubled in size.

Bake bread in a preheated 375° oven for 40 minutes or until cooked through. To test, thump or knock on the loaf; it will sound hollow when done. The loaf will have a crusty exterior and a golden color. Cooking time will vary with the size loaf made.

— *Thierry Tellier, Pastry Chef, la Madeleine*

Bread from Nice
Pain de Nice

Preparation: 30 minutes, plus
   1¼ hours rising time
Cooking: 45 minutes
Yield: 4 (1-pound) loaves
Equipment: mixer, 6-quart bowl,
   bread pans

INGREDIENTS

1½ packages dry yeast plus
   3 tablespoons lukewarm water
   (105–115°)
3⅓ cups whole wheat flour
   (16 ounces)
6¾ cups all-purpose flour
   (32 ounces)
5 teaspoons salt (1 ounce)
2 tablespoons extra virgin olive
   oil
2–3 cups water
½ cup carrot, peeled and cut in
   julienne or grated
½ cup turnip, peeled and cut in
   julienne
½ cup onion, peeled and cut in
   julienne or chopped
½ cup leek (white part only), cut
   in julienne
1 bunch of parsley, stems
   removed and chopped
3 tablespoons unsalted butter
   (to grease bowl and pans)

Very popular in Provence, this bread is unusual because it is loaded with pieces of vegetables. It makes great ham sandwiches. It is a wonderful accompaniment to any soup or salad. But those who really understand and appreciate good bread may prefer to eat Bread from Nice by itself.

Sprinkle dry yeast over 3 tablespoons lukewarm water. Set aside for 5 minutes in a warm place to proof. Mixture will become foamy as the yeast begins working. Then add flours, salt, extra virgin olive oil, and enough water to make a soft dough.

Knead about 5 minutes at medium speed in a mixer with a dough hook and add the vegetables and parsley. Continue mixing, just until combined. Transfer dough to a greased bowl, cover loosely with a towel, and set aside in a warm place. Let dough rise until doubled, about 45 minutes.

Punch down to expel gases from dough and form into desired loaf shapes. Use standard bread pans or shape into round loaves. Grease bread molds with butter or oil and place dough in the molds to rise for 30 more minutes, or until doubled in size.

Bake in preheated 375° oven for 45 minutes or until done. Turn bread out onto a rack to cool.

— Thierry Tellier, Pastry Chef, la Madeleine

French Maxim—As we travel along, the wonderful aroma of fresh bread will make us detour to wherever the bread is baking.

Spinach and Sausage Bread
Pain aux Epinards et à la Saucisse

Preparation: 35 minutes, plus
   1 hour rising time
Cooking: 20 minutes (Filling),
   35 minutes (Bread)
Yield: 4 loaves
Equipment: mixer, bowls,
   12-inch sauté pan, rolling pin,
   13-inch x 18-inch baking sheet

INGREDIENTS

1 cup milk
4 tablespoons unsalted butter
2 tablespoons sugar
1 tablespoon salt
2 packages dry yeast plus l cup
   lukewarm water (105–115°)
6½ cups sifted all-purpose or
   bread flour
8 ounces freshly grated
   Parmesan cheese, divided use
1 egg
1 tablespoon water

FILLING

1 pound hot Italian sausage
2 (10-ounce) packages chopped
   spinach, thawed
2 large eggs
Salt to taste
Freshly ground pepper to taste
Red pepper flakes to taste

A combination of sausage and spinach makes this a hearty loaf with a soft crust. It is guaranteed to be a hit at your next picnic, delicious when served with wine, cheese, and fruit. The bread can be sliced on an angle and served as an appetizer, or it can be fashioned into the shape of breadsticks. It freezes well and is well worth the effort it takes to create.

Prepare homemade bread. Heat the milk. Remove from heat and stir in unsalted butter, sugar, and salt. Cool to lukewarm. Meanwhile, stir yeast into lukewarm water in a large bowl. When yeast is completely dissolved, stir in the milk mixture. Gradually stir in about three cups of flour. Mix well and then beat with a spoon for 1 minute. Add all but ½ cup of remaining flour and mix well, using your hands if necessary. Sprinkle remaining ½ cup of flour on a board. Turn dough out onto board and knead it for about 10 minutes, or until dough becomes very smooth, elastic, and satiny. Grease a large bowl generously. Place dough in the bowl, then turn it over so the entire surface is lightly greased. Cover bowl with a damp cloth and put it in a warm, draft-free place. Let dough rise until doubled, about 45 minutes.

Prepare filling. First, brown sausage in a skillet. Drain and squeeze extra water from spinach. Add spinach to browned sausage and cook until all moisture is gone. Remove from heat. Add 2 eggs, salt, pepper, and red pepper flakes to taste. Stir well. Set aside until ready to use.

Punch bread dough down and flatten it on a floured board, cutting dough into four equal parts. With a rolling pin roll each piece into a rectangle of about 6 inches x 14 inches. Spread ¼ of sausage/spinach mixture on dough, ½ inch from the edges. Sprinkle each filling with 2 ounces of shredded Parmesan cheese. Roll, starting with the 14-inch side of the dough, jelly roll style. Pinch seams and ends and place seam side down on baking stone or sheet. Allow about 3 inches between each loaf. Let rise until doubled in size. Brush a beaten mixture of 1 egg and 1 tablespoon water on each loaf. Bake in a preheated 350° oven for 25 to 35 minutes or until a light golden brown. To test, thump or knock on loaf; it will sound hollow when done.

—*Denise Wyant, la Madeleine*

Reci Tip—Before cutting fresh bread, put the blade of the knife in boiling water and dry.

SALADS

Hot Duck Salad Château de la Marchère
Salade de Canard Chaude de la Marchère

Salad from Southern France
Salade du Midi de la France

Pepper Salad
Salade de Poivrons

Winter Salad
Salade d'Hiver

la Madeleine Caesar Salad

Zucchini Salad with Mushrooms
Salade de Courgettes aux Champignons

Chicken Salad with Almonds
Salade de Poulet aux Amandes

Grand Duchess Salad
Salade Grande Duchesse

Vinaigrettes

Hot Duck Salad Château de la Marchère
Salade de Canard Chaude de la Marchère

Preparation: 20 minutes
Cooking: 15 minutes
Servings: 4
Equipment: 1½-quart saucepan,
  12-inch skillet

INGREDIENTS

8 ounces curly lettuce (frisee,
  mustard, radicchio, curly leaf,
  escarole, endive, or Boston)
8 new potatoes
2 duck breasts or filets, or 4
  thighs
2 tablespoons extra virgin olive
  oil
2½ tablespoons unsalted butter
5 ounces bacon, sliced
¾–1 cup Basic Vinaigrette
  (p. 51)
1 clove garlic, minced
1 shallot, minced
¼ cup minced parsley, divided
  use
4 ounces red lettuce leaves
Salt to taste
Freshly ground pepper to taste

This recipe comes from Château de la Marchère, a fifteenth-century manor that was involved in the Hundred Years War that stormed across the French countryside. Today it is a charming place, thanks to the care of Annie Leddet, whose sense of her family's traditions makes history come alive. Her Hot Duck Salad reminds us of Touraine's celebrated hunting and is especially satisfying for a crisp fall lunch.

Wrap washed lettuce leaves in a towel and chill in the refrigerator. Cook potatoes in salted water about 20 minutes or until tender. Cool under running water, peel, and cut into ¼-inch slices.

Season duck with salt and pepper. Score the skin and cook in a skillet over moderate heat in the olive oil and butter, 10 minutes on each side. Wrap cooked duck in foil to keep warm, and set aside. In the same skillet, sauté bacon until crisp. Drain on paper, cut into squares, and set aside with the duck.

Add garlic, shallots, and 2 tablespoons of the parsley to the Basic Vinaigrette and mix well. Toss lettuce with some of the dressing. Slice duck about the same thickness as the potatoes.

To serve, toss lettuce with some of the prepared Vinaigrette and arrange on plates. Alternate slices of duck with slices of potato on the lettuce and sprinkle with the bacon. Surround with red lettuce and garnish with the remaining 2 tablespoons of parsley.

—Annie Leddet, Château de la Marchère

Reci Tip—If salad greens are getting a little old and wilted, put them in warm water, then rinse them in cold water. They will become fresh and crisp.

—Danielle Renard

Salad from Southern France

Salade du Midi de la France

Preparation: 12 minutes
Cooking: 15 minutes
Servings: 4
Equipment: sharp knife, shallow
  10-inch to 12-inch oven dish

INGREDIENTS

4 medium zucchini (about 1½
  pounds)
4 tomatoes (about 1½ pounds)
¼ cup extra virgin olive oil,
  divided use
Salt to taste
Freshly ground pepper to taste
4 sprigs thyme
½ cup Basic or Pungent Vinaigrette (p. 51)
¼ cup chopped fresh parsley, or
  2 tablespoons dried
¼ cup snipped fresh basil leaves,
  or 2 tablespoons dried
16 Calamata olives, pitted

This pretty summer salad with flavorful tomatoes has the distinct taste of Southern France. When served with toasted whole grain bread and goat cheese, it makes a nice light meal.

Preheat oven to 375°. Slice zucchini in ⅜-inch rounds.

Slice tomatoes the same thickness as the zucchini. If tomatoes are large, cut in half to produce slices more like the shape of zucchini.

Grease an ovenproof dish with 2 tablespoons olive oil and overlap alternate slices of zucchini and tomato. Sprinkle with remaining olive oil and season with salt, pepper, and thyme. Bake for 15 minutes.

To serve, turn out on a plate and season with ½ cup Vinaigrette. Garnish with chopped parsley, basil, and olives. Or serve in oven dish with Vinaigrette on the side.

French Maxim—A husband and wife who enjoy good food together—at least once each day—will love longer.

Pepper Salad
Salade de Poivrons

Très Simple

Preparation: 15 minutes, plus 30
 minutes refrigeration
Cooking: 30 minutes
Serves: 4
Equipment: 1-quart saucepan,
 3-quart mixing bowl, salad
 platter

INGREDIENTS

¼ cup wild rice
1 cup boiling water
2 large bell peppers, any color
2 large tomatoes,
1 apple, peeled, cored, and diced
4 large lettuce leaves (Boston,
 red, or romaine)
1 red or white onion, peeled and
 cut into rings
1 small bunch parsley

INGREDIENTS

4 tablespoons heavy cream
4 tablespoons extra virgin olive
 oil
½ teaspoon curry powder
½ teaspoon powdered cumin
Salt to taste
Freshly ground pepper to taste

Yield: ½ cup

Unusual and vividly colored, especially with a variety of peppers, this salad has the visual impact of an artist's palette. Toss the apple with some lemon juice to prevent browning if not serving right away.

Cook rice in boiling salted water for 14 minutes; drain and chill.

Broil peppers until the skin turns black. Cool in paper bag and peel. Dice and set aside.

Peel tomatoes, cut in half and squeeze gently in order to remove any excess liquid and the seeds. Cut tomatoes into small pieces. Peel, core, and dice apples. Mix together cold rice, peppers, tomatoes, and apples. Season mixture with Curry Dressing. Arrange salad on lettuce leaves in a deep platter. Rinse onion slices well in ice water. Dry and use as a garnish with sprigs of parsley.

Curry Dressing

Whisk together all of the ingredients until combined. Additional curry powder or cumin may be added as desired. If making dressing ahead of time, refrigerate until use.

Winter Salad
Salade d'Hiver

Très Simple

Preparation: 15 minutes
Cooking: 30 minutes
Servings: 4
Equipment: 1-quart saucepan,
  knife, salad platter

INGREDIENTS

1 large or several small red beets
  (½–¾ pound)
2 Belgian endives
2 Golden Delicious apples
5 ounces Gruyère cheese
2 tablespoons pine nuts
1 tablespoon white or brown
  raisins
Salt to taste
Freshly ground pepper to taste
¾ cup Fruit Vinaigrette (p. 51)

When you want a bright, colorful salad to accompany soup, consider the salad that was designed to add cheer to any winter night. It is equally great as an accompaniment to Chicken for a Winter Sunday (p. 67) or Braised Beef (p. 77). The variety of Gruyère known as Comté is the best in this salad.

Preheat oven to 350°. Wrap beet in foil and bake until tender, about 30 minutes. Plunge into cold water. Peel beet and dice into ½-inch cubes.

Clean and separate endive leaves; set aside.

Peel apples and remove seeds; cut into quarters if small or dice into ½-inch cubes if large. Toss apples with some Fruit Vinaigrette, if not using immediately, to prevent browning.

Cut cheese into very small cubes. Set aside. Toast pine nuts for 10 minutes at 350°.

Arrange endive leaves in the form of a star on a platter. In the center, arrange cheese, diced beet, raisins, and apple quarters. Season with salt and pepper to taste. Pour Fruit Vinaigrette over the mixture. Garnish top with pine nuts.

Alternatively, toss everything together except the endives. The mixture will be a rosy pink color. Serve mounded on the endive "star."

Reci Tip—If you spill a drop of red wine on your clothes, just dab white wine on the spot and rub it out.
—Monique Felzine

*A quiet and thoughtful gardener especially in the way he nurtured his children,
François Esquerré, Patrick Esquerré's father, is equally able with his floral charges.*

*Château les Pins was also a working farm that surrounded the Esquerré family
with the freshness and simplicity—and wonderful tastes—of a life lived close to nature.*

The milk house was the cottage where
François and Monique Esquerré raised their children.

Annie Leddet, a long-time friend from
Château de la Marchère, exchanges recipes
with Monique Esquerré (right).

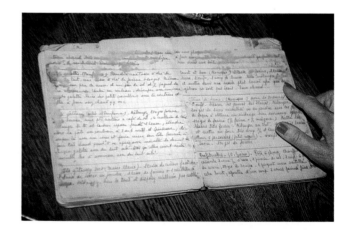

This is Patrick's great-great grandmother Mère Loulou's
handwritten cookbook, containing the Esquerré recipes that
have been passed down from one generation to the next.

Patrick Esquerré in tune with the la Madeleine family.

Stanley Marcus contributed his own special magic to the creation of la Madeleine.

Julia Child and a friend.

Clockwise from upper left: Carrot Soup with Tomatoes (p. 32);
Chilled Cucumber Soup (p. 33); and Brie Soup (p. 31)

Jean-Luc's Pot-au-Feu de Légumes (p. 140)

Gruyère Cheese Straws (p. 59)

la Madeleine Caesar Salad (p. 47)

Peasant-Style Soup (p. 35)

Hot Duck Salad Château de la Marchère (p. 43)

la Madeleine Caesar Salad

Preparation: 20 minutes
Cooking: not required
Servings: 4
Equipment: salad bowl

INGREDIENTS

6 ounces romaine lettuce
   (2 quarts)
6 ounces green leaf lettuce
   (about 2 quarts)
8 ounces grated Parmesan
   cheese (about 2 cups)
1 cup la Madeleine Croutons
1 cup la Madeleine Caesar
   Dressing

This, of course, is the popular Caesar Salad of la Madeleine. The bakeries are presently serving thousands of salads a day, and now you can bring the Caesar Salad to your own table. We are happy to share what we can about the salad, but, unfortunately, we made a promise years ago not to divulge the secrets in the dressing. If you use the la Madeleine dressing, the shelf life of the dressing is four weeks. Keep it refrigerated, since it contains no preservatives. If you don't have a la Madeleine bakery in your area, try making the Sherry Vinaigrette (p. 52), but substitute red wine vinegar for the sherry wine vinegar.

Wash and dry romaine and leaf lettuce and cut into bite-size pieces, about ½ inch. Wrap in a towel, then a plastic bag, and chill, if necessary, until serving.

To serve, mix lettuce in a large salad bowl with Parmesan cheese and croutons. Toss lightly. (Parmesan cheese refers to Parmigiano Reggiano, a cheese manufactured in the province of Parma, Italy, and allowed to mature from one to ten years. It is preferable to grate just before using.)

Add salad dressing and toss lightly until combined. Serve immediately.
                                        —la Madeleine

Croutons

INGREDIENTS

4 cups bread cubes, cut from
   day-old bread
¼ cup extra virgin olive oil
2 cloves garlic, minced

Yield: 1 quart

Preheat oven to 350°. Cut day-old bread into cubes or sticks. Place in a bowl and mix with olive oil and garlic. Spread on a cookie sheet and bake about 15 minutes until brown. Toss occasionally to prevent burning. When cool, store in airtight container.

Zucchini Salad with Mushrooms
Salade de Courgettes aux Champignons

Très Simple

Preparation: 15 minutes
Cooking: not required
Servings: 4
Equipment: grater or knife,
  2-quart bowl, salad plates

INGREDIENTS

½ cup Pungent Vinaigrette
  (p. 51)
1 tablespoon Dijon mustard
3 zucchini (about 1½ pounds)
1 onion, peeled and finely
  chopped
4 large mushrooms
1 tablespoon chopped chives
1 tablespoon snipped basil
2 medium tomatoes, cut into
  eighths
8 basil leaves

When you want to serve a salad that is simple to make but beautiful, try this Zucchini Salad with Mushrooms. It is delicious. It is artful. For a party, pack each serving of the zucchini into an espresso coffee cup and turn out onto plates for a "formed" look. Surround with mushrooms and place tomato eighths around like spokes in a wheel.

Add an additional tablespoon of Dijon mustard to the Pungent Vinaigrette recipe to thicken.

Wash zucchini and cut into thin julienne strips, or grate. Season with some of the Vinaigrette (about 4 tablespoons). Add the onion.

Wash mushrooms and dice. Season with remainder of the Vinaigrette, chives, and basil.

Arrange zucchini mixture in the middle of individual plates. Sprinkle chopped mushrooms around the salad and garnish with tomato eighths and fresh basil leaves.

French Maxim—Gastronomy is the art of eating well without eating more than we need.

Chicken Salad with Almonds
Salade de Poulet aux Amandes

Preparation: 30 minutes
Cooking: 1 hour
Servings: 6
Equipment: 6-quart stockpot,
   3-quart mixing bowl

INGREDIENTS

1¾ ounces white raisins
1 bunch watercress or lettuce
1 whole chicken (3–4 pounds),
   cooked, cooled, and deboned
3 ribs celery, diced
4 ounces almonds, blanched or
   slivered
1½ cups mayonnaise
Pinch paprika
Juice of 1 lemon
Salt to taste
Freshly ground pepper to taste
Lemon slices for garnish
Parsley sprigs for garnish

The unexpected combination of watercress and raisins makes this salad a delightful, tasty addition to a party or a summertime picnic. You can make the salad ahead, but wait and add the watercress at the last moment.

Rinse raisins in cold water. Allow them to soak and swell in a bowl of warm water for 1–2 hours. Drain and dry them on paper towels and set aside.

Cut watercress or lettuce into ½-inch pieces, wrap in towels, and refrigerate until serving.

Cut cooked chicken (or use leftover chicken) into small pieces and place in a large salad bowl. Add celery, watercress, almonds, and raisins.

Season mayonnaise with paprika, lemon juice, salt, and pepper. Check seasoning.

Mix all ingredients together and serve. Garnish with half-rounds of lemon and sprigs of parsley.

Reci Tip—If your oven has a tendency to dry out your chicken, put a saucer of water in the oven while the chicken is baking.

Grand Duchess Salad

Salade Grande Duchesse

Preparation: 20 minutes
Cooking: 30 minutes
Servings: 4
Equipment: 3-quart saucepan,
 sharp knife, 3-quart bowl

INGREDIENTS

2 pounds new potatoes
6 ounces extra fine French-style
 green beans*
3 ribs celery, julienned
1 cup mayonnaise, thinned with
 1 tablespoon lemon juice
Salt to taste
Freshly ground pepper to taste
½ cup Basic Vinaigrette (p. 51)
7 ounces curly lettuce
¼ cup chervil or ¼ cup parsley,
 chopped

*If French green beans (haricots
 verts) are not available, substitute regular ones, cut to size.

A relative who invented this recipe traveled around France pretending she was a genuine duchess with royal blood flowing in her veins. Since everyone believed her, this dish is called Grand Duchess Salad. Both her life and her salad were great inventions.

Boil potatoes until just cooked, about 20 minutes. Do not over-cook potatoes or they will not slice evenly. Drain, cool in a bowl of water, and drain again. Peel and slice to the same size as the beans (about ¼ inch; a mandoline would be helpful here). Cook beans in slightly salted water for 5 minutes. Drain, cool in a bowl of water, and drain again.

Mix beans (reserve ¼ cup for garnish), celery, and potatoes. Add mayonnaise and mix well. Season with salt and pepper.

Season lettuce with Vinaigrette and arrange at the edge of plates. Turn vegetable mixture out in the center of the plates. Sprinkle with chervil or parsley and reserved green beans.

In the winter you could substitute celery root for the celery. Peel, julienne, and toss with some lemon juice or Vinaigrette to prevent discoloring.

Reci Tip—Parsley has long been known to ensure longevity. A
 French centenarian credited her perfect physique
 with the fact she had consumed, during her life-
 time, the equivalent of four acres of parsley and
 twenty tons of lemons.

Vinaigrettes

Très Simple

All recipes yield approximately
1 cup

BASIC VINAIGRETTE

⅓ cup vinegar
Salt to taste
Freshly ground pepper to taste
⅔ cup extra virgin olive oil

PUNGENT VINAIGRETTE

3 tablespoons vinegar
1 tablespoon Dijon-style
    mustard or 1 teaspoon dry
    mustard
Freshly ground pepper to taste
¾ cup extra virgin olive oil

FRUIT VINAIGRETTE

⅓ cup apple cider vinegar or
    another fruit-flavored vinegar
Salt to taste
Freshly ground pepper to taste
⅔ cup nut oil (walnut, hazelnut,
    peanut) or use equal amounts
    nut and canola oil for a lighter
    flavor

The basis of any good salad lies in the quality and freshness of the ingredients. Proper technique and handling will assure success. Lettuce should be washed, dried, and crisped in the refrigerator between layers of towels prior to serving. Only the best oils and vinegars should be used: extra virgin olive oil (first press or cold press), canola oil, walnut oil, or hazelnut oil. The choice of vinegar is essential and the flavor varies with its composition. This is the key element in the flavoring of the Vinaigrette. The vinegars could be red or white wine vinegar, sherry, balsamic, fruit, herb, or just an acid such as lemon juice. Proportions vary to achieve a variety of flavors. The third component of flavoring is mustard. In France there are one hundred kinds of mustards used to vary the taste and flavor of vinaigrettes. Experiment with the ingredients and mixtures to achieve your favorite dressing. The addition of fresh herbs is appropriate in any of the dressings.

Place vinegar, salt, pepper, and any other seasonings (including mustard or egg yolk) in a bowl.

Whisk ingredients until salt is dissolved. Slowly add oil while whisking constantly. Dressing should thicken.

At this point garlic, shallots, chopped egg, herbs, capers, cheese, or other seasonings may be added.

(continued on following page)

SHERRY VINAIGRETTE

2 tablespoons sherry wine
    vinegar
Juice of 1 lemon
1 egg yolk, very fresh (or 1 table-
    spoon of Dijon-style mustard
    to help emulsify the dressing)
Salt to taste
Freshly ground pepper to taste
6 tablespoons canola or peanut
    oil
4 tablespoons extra virgin olive
    oil

Vinaigrettes will keep 1–2 weeks in the refrigerator. Re-blend at serving time. If using egg in a Vinaigrette, select very fresh eggs, store dressing in refrigerator, and use within one day.

VINAIGRETTE ZERO
(NO OIL/NO FAT)

4 ounces tomato juice
Juice of 1 lemon
1 small onion, peeled and minced
1 teaspoon chopped parsley
2 teaspoons mustard
Salt to taste
Freshly ground pepper to taste

Combine all ingredients and mix well with a whisk. Other herbs may be used in this Vinaigrette depending on availability. This Vinaigrette may be used for any salad or vegetable.

FIRST COURSES

Small Hot Ham Turnovers
Petits Pâtés de Jambon Chauds

Ham Terrine
Terrine de Jambon

Vegetable Terrine
Terrine de Légumes

Marbled Eggs
Les Oeufs Marbrés au Thé

Gruyère Cheese Straws
Les Allumettes au Gruyère

Red Bell Pepper Bavarois
Bavarois de Poivrons Rouges

Salmon Rillettes
Rillettes de Saumon

Small Hot Ham Turnovers
Petits Pâtés de Jambon Chauds

Preparation: 25 minutes
Cooking: 15 minutes
Servings: 8–10
Equipment: food processor or
    knife, rolling pin, 12-inch
    skillet, pastry brush,
    13-inch x 18-inch baking sheet

INGREDIENTS

8 ounces mushrooms
1 tablespoon unsalted butter
Salt to taste
Freshly ground white pepper to
    taste
½ pound smoked ham
1 cup Béchamel Sauce (p. 91)
2 egg yolks
Chervil, minced, to taste
Tarragon, minced, to taste
1 pound Puff Pastry Dough,
    (pp. 131–32) or substitute
    frozen puff pastry

EGG WASH

1 egg yolk
1 teaspoon milk

These are well worth the effort, delicate yet full of flavor. Take them along on a picnic, pack in a lunch box, or serve with soup. Make smaller ones to serve as a first course before one of the braised meats or Champagne Chicken (p. 66).

Remove and discard discolored portion of mushroom stems. Wash mushrooms well in water containing a small amount of vinegar, drain, and dry them well. Mince mushrooms and sauté in butter 5–6 minutes over medium high heat. Season with salt and pepper. Cook longer, if necessary, to eliminate liquid in the pan. The mushrooms should be fairly dry. Preheat oven to 450°.

Finely chop ham in a food mill, a food processor, or with a knife. In a bowl thoroughly mix together minced ham, mushrooms, Béchamel Sauce, 2 egg yolks, chervil, and tarragon. Check seasoning, adding salt and pepper if necessary.

In a small bowl, beat remaining egg yolk with milk and set aside. On a well-floured surface roll out dough and cut out 6-inch squares. Fill them with 2 tablespoons of stuffing mixture, placing the filling to the right of center. Brush a narrow strip of egg yolk mixture around the entire edge, then fold the left side over and seal by gently pressing with fingertips. Place on a baking sheet that has been lightly greased or lined with parchment paper. Brush surface with egg yolk mixture.

Bake for 15 minutes or until puffed and golden brown. Serve warm.

These small pies can be kept in the freezer and reheated in oven at 375° for 20 minutes prior to serving.

Ham Terrine
Terrine de Jambon

Très Simple

Preparation: 25 minutes
Cooking: 40 minutes
Servings: 6
Equipment: 3-quart bowl,
   2-quart loaf pan, parchment
   paper, bowl

INGREDIENTS

3 eggs
1¼ cups all-purpose flour
1 teaspoon baking powder
½ cup milk
¼ cup extra virgin olive oil
½ cup grated Swiss cheese
12 ounces ham or cooked garlic
   sausage (about 2 cups), diced
½ cup black olives (optional)
Salt to taste
Freshly ground pepper to taste
1 tablespoon snipped chives
1 tablespoon snipped fresh
   tarragon
Nutmeg to taste
Unsalted butter for pan

Ham Terrine, a unique and easy recipe, was contributed by Monique Binet, the Maîtresse de Maison, an excellent cook. Her skillful balance of the duties of cook and of hostess are a perfect combination for her fortunate guests.

Preheat oven to 400°.

In a bowl, beat the eggs with a whisk. Add flour and baking powder, whisking until thick. Then gradually add milk, olive oil, and cheese. Add ham or cooked sausage and olives, if using. Add salt, pepper, chives, tarragon, and nutmeg to taste.

Cut parchment paper to fit the loaf pan. Butter the pan and the paper and line pan with parchment paper. Pour mixture into the prepared pan and bake for 40 minutes. Test the terrine with a knife to see if it has cooked through. Allow to cool slightly and turn out of pan onto a plate. Slice to serve.

—*Monique Binet, Hôtesse Extraordinaire*

French Maxim—The secret to keeping a family at home is to feed its members well, especially the spouse.

Vegetable Terrine
Terrine de Légumes

Preparation: 30 minutes
Cooking: 1½ hours
Servings: 8
Equipment: 6-quart saucepan, colander, slotted spoon, blender, 3-quart loaf pan or terrine

INGREDIENTS

½ pound cauliflower florets
1½ pounds broccoli florets, divided use
6 eggs
¾ cup heavy cream
Salt to taste
Freshly ground pepper to taste
¼ cup fresh herbs, minced (parsley, tarragon, Mexican mint marigold, or basil)
¼ pound shredded or grated carrots

INGREDIENTS

2 cups half-and-half
1 cup chopped parsley
½ cup chopped chervil
½ cup snipped chives
Salt to taste
Freshly ground pepper to taste

Yield: 3 cups

Slice Vegetable Terrine and serve it as a first course with Herb Sauce or tomato sauce. It is a tasty addition to any meal, but the terrine and the beautiful Herb Sauce are especially delicious with grilled chicken or fish.

Blanch cauliflower and half of broccoli in boiling, salted water for 2 minutes. Remove vegetables with a slotted spoon and plunge into cold water to stop cooking and to brighten the color. Drain in a colander. Cook remaining broccoli for 5 minutes, or until soft. Remove broccoli with slotted spoon and plunge into cold water. Drain in a colander. Put the second batch of broccoli in a blender or food processor and blend well with eggs, cream, salt, pepper, and fresh herbs. Mixture will be green.

Preheat oven to 350°. Butter an ovenproof terrine or loaf pan. Place blanched broccoli and cauliflower and the carrots in the pan. Pour the blended broccoli/egg mixture over the vegetables. Mix slightly to distribute the vegetables evenly. Bake terrine for 1 hour 15 minutes. Cooking is complete when a knife inserted into the center comes out clean. Unmold, slice, and serve warm.

Herb Sauce

Pour half-and-half into a saucepan and add fresh, chopped herbs. Cook over low heat about 10 minutes or until slightly reduced and the consistency of a sauce. Transfer mixture to a blender and purée. Season with salt and pepper. Serve as is or strain for a smoother sauce.

—Jean Bardet

Marbled Eggs
Les Oeufs Marbrés au Thé

Très Simple

Preparation: 10 minutes, plus
  1 hour to chill
Cooking: 12 minutes
Yield: 12 eggs
Equipment: 6-quart saucepan,
  slotted spoon, pastry bag
  (optional)

INGREDIENTS

12 eggs
3 tablespoons smoky Chinese tea
  leaves, such as Lapsang
  souchong
4 tablespoons minced parsley
4 tablespoons minced chives or
  tarragon
Mayonnaise to taste
Optional toppings (see sugges-
  tions in recipe introduction)

The surprising marbled effect makes these eggs a real conversation piece, the talk of any party. Be creative and garnish the eggs with other delicacies such as shrimp, smoked salmon, caviar, asparagus, carrot, or pepper. For a neater egg, use a pastry bag to pipe on the mayonnaise when serving halves upright. Or cut the eggs in half lengthwise and place the cut sides down, spoke fashion. Put mayonnaise and herbs in the center.

Place eggs in saucepan and cover with water. Boil, reduce heat, and simmer 5 minutes. Remove eggs with a slotted spoon. Plunge eggs into cold water, cooling them enough to handle.

Using the flat side of a knife blade, gently crack eggshells over the entire surface. Do not peel eggs. Keep water boiling in saucepan and add tea leaves.

Return eggs to water and cook for 7 minutes. Remove pan from heat and allow eggs to cool, still immersed in tea water. Place the eggs in the refrigerator—still in their tea water—to help prevent dark lines on the yolk. Chill for 1 hour.

Remove egg shells. Eggs now have a marbled effect. Cut eggs in half to serve. Garnish with herbs. Serve with mayonnaise.

Reci Tip—If you want your eggs colored with natural dyes, dilute saffron in water for orange, boil an onion peel for yellow, boil spinach juice for green, or beet juice for red.

Gruyère Cheese Straws
Les Allumettes au Gruyère

Preparation: 30 minutes
Cooking: 12–15 minutes
Servings: 9–12
Equipment: bowl, 13-inch x 18-inch baking pan, rolling pin, knife or pizza wheel, pastry brush

INGREDIENTS

2 teaspoons milk
10 tablespoons unsalted butter, softened
1½ cups grated Gruyère cheese (about 6 ounces)
Freshly ground white pepper to taste
1 cup flour
½ teaspoon salt
Extra grated Gruyère cheese or caraway seeds (optional)

EGG WASH

1 egg yolk
1 teaspoon milk

Each time the Esquerré family had visitors, these cheese straws were served with wine before dinner. They became so popular that we always wondered if our guests had come to see us or merely to partake of the cheese straws. Fragile and crispy, they will melt in your mouth.

In a mixing bowl, using a wooden spoon mix together milk, butter, cheese, and pepper. Stir in flour and salt, blending thoroughly to obtain a smooth dough. Roll dough into a ball, flatten slightly and wrap in wax paper. Chill dough for 30 minutes in the refrigerator.

Preheat oven to 450°.

Roll out dough on a floured surface in the form of an elongated rectangle, approximately 8 inches x 4 inches. Cut into strips approximately ¼-inch x 4 inches. To help reduce spreading, chill the cut dough again for 30 minutes. Place strips on a buttered or parchment-lined baking pan, allowing a 2-inch space between the "straws."

Whisk together egg yolk and milk; brush the strips with mixture. Sprinkle with grated Gruyère cheese or caraway seeds.

Bake for 12–15 minutes until lightly brown on top. Remove from pan with a spatula and transfer to a rack to cool. Arrange on a paper doily and serve warm.

French Maxim—A meal without cheese is like a friend without a smile.

Red Bell Pepper Bavarois
Bavarois de Poivrons Rouges

Preparation: 15 minutes, plus 3
   hours refrigeration
Cooking: 30 minutes
Servings: 9–12
Equipment: 6-quart saucepan
   with cover, molds, blender

INGREDIENTS

4½ pounds red bell peppers
2½ cups dry white wine, divided
   use
½ cup brandy
2¼ cups water
3 garlic cloves, chopped
3 shallots, chopped
Salt to taste
Freshly ground white pepper to
   taste
3 envelopes unflavored gelatin
2 cups heavy cream (optional)
Unsalted butter or extra virgin
   olive oil for molds
Fresh Tomato Sauce (p. 91)
Parsley, chopped, for garnish
Basil or lettuce leaves (optional)
1 baguette, sliced (optional)

Vary the color of the peppers, creating a versatile, vividly
colored first course, especially during the summertime,
when gardens provide a lush bounty of vegetables. If you make
a red pepper mold, a yellow tomato coulis offers a nice contrast. The cream in the recipe can be omitted for a satisfying
fat-free appetizer.

Seed peppers and chop in large pieces. Combine peppers, 2
cups white wine, brandy, water, garlic, shallots, salt, and pepper
in a saucepan. Bring to a boil, reduce heat, cover, and simmer
for 30 minutes.

Soften powdered gelatin in ½ cup wine in a bowl. Place container in simmering water, stirring to dissolve.

Transfer the pepper mixture to a blender. Reduce liquid
remaining in the pan, if necessary, to about 2 tablespoons and
add to blender. Purée. Add dissolved gelatin to hot purée with
the blender motor running. After blending well, allow purée to
cool slightly. Add some thick or lightly whipped cream to give
purée a heavier consistency, if desired.

Butter or oil molds and fill them with the pepper purée. Refrigerate for at least 3 hours or overnight to firm.

To serve, dip molds in hot water, if necessary, and unmold on
individual serving plates. Garnish with chopped parsley, fresh
basil, or lettuce leaves. Serve as a salad or as a spread for sliced
baguettes.

Salmon Rillettes
Rillettes de Saumon

Preparation: 10 minutes
Cooking: 20 minutes
Servings: 4
Equipment: 8-inch skillet, knife,
   2-cup terrine or bowl

INGREDIENTS

1 10-ounce salmon fillet, 1 inch
   thick
2 8-ounce peppered smoked
   mackerel filets
6 shallots, chopped
5 sprigs cilantro, chopped
1 cup dry white wine
2 tablespoons chopped fresh
   chervil
2 tablespoons snipped fresh
   chives
Salt to taste
Freshly ground pepper to taste
Additional uncut chervil and
   chives for garnish
1 baguette, sliced

Lou Salmon is constantly inventing recipes that get better and better as time goes by. She is blessed with great common sense, which is the number-one quality of a good cook. Her Salmon Rillettes reflect her culinary talents, especially when served with a French baguette or crackers and a chilled white wine. Peppered smoked mackerel is easily available and adds a wonderful flavor.

Wipe salmon with a damp cloth. Remove skin from the smoked mackerel, and break meat into very small pieces, discarding any bones.

Spread shallots in a small skillet. Cover with cilantro. Place salmon on top and pour wine over. Poach gently, uncovered, for 7–10 minutes, turning once.

Break cooked salmon into very small pieces, discarding the skin and bones. Mix mackerel, salmon, cooking liquid, and chopped herbs in a bowl. Season with salt and pepper. Pack mixture into a terrine. Garnish with uncut herbs, cover, and chill. Serve with a sliced baguette.

—*Lou Salmon*

ENTRÉES

Tarragon Chicken
Poulet à l' Estragon

Champagne Chicken
Poulet au Champagne

Chicken for a Winter Sunday
Poule-au-Pot d'un Dimanche Hivernal

Chicken with Lemons
Poulet au Citron

Quail with Red Bell Peppers
Cailles aux Poivrons Rouges

Pheasant in a Pot
Faisan en Cocotte

Stuffed Family-Style Veal Scallop
Escalope Familiale Farcie

Agnes Sorel Veal Delights
Delices Agnes Sorel

Veal Filet Mignon
Mignon de Veau à la Salomon

Beef in Shallot Sauce
Tournedos en Sauce Echalote

Pot-au-Feu

Braised Beef
Boeuf Braisé

Pork Roast with Oranges
Porc à l'Orange

Lamb Stew with Fresh Spring Vegetables
Navarin aux Petits Légumes Nouveaux

Cassoulet

Aunt Alice's Pie
Pâté de Tante Alice

Oysters in a Bowl
Cassolette d'Huitres à l'Impromptu

Trout with Chives
Truite à la Ciboulette

Salmon in Parchment
Saumon en Papillote

Filet of Sole and Salmon Braised in Cream
Paupiettes de Sole et Saumon Braisées à la Crème

Scallops on a Skewer
Brochettes de Coquilles Saint-Jacques

Stocks and Sauces

Bordeaux Wine Sauce
Sauce au Bordeaux

Extra Virgin Tomato Sauce

Fresh Tomato Sauce
Coulis de Tomates

Béchamel Sauce

Tarragon Chicken
Poulet à l'Estragon

Très Simple

Preparation: 10 minutes
Cooking: 60–70 minutes
Servings: 4
Equipment: shallow roasting pan
   or cocotte, 1-quart saucepan,
   kitchen string

INGREDIENTS

1 3½–4-pound chicken
Salt to taste
Freshly ground pepper to taste
3 sprigs tarragon, plus 2 tablespoons chopped
Oil or unsalted butter
1 tablespoon tarragon-flavored
   mustard
1 cup heavy cream
Additional tarragon sprigs for
   garnish

The timeless marriage of chicken and tarragon is unrivaled in this classic recipe that everyone will love. If tarragon is not available, you can substitute another fresh herb. Mexican mint marigold will give you about the same flavor. Tarragon Chicken can be served with both Carrot Purée (p. 99) and Parisian Potatoes (p. 104). If you leave off the sauce, you have the basic recipe for roast chicken. You may want to cook an extra chicken, perhaps for Chicken Salad with Almonds (p. 49).

Preheat the oven to 400°.

Salt and pepper interior of the chicken and add 3 sprigs of tarragon. Coat the exterior with oil (to make the skin more crackling) and lightly oil the bottom of the pan. Truss chicken. Roast chicken on its side in a 400° oven for 60–70 minutes, turning the chicken when it is brown on one side, after about 30 minutes.

Remove cooked chicken to a platter and cover loosely with foil. Skim fat from pan juices and pour into a saucepan. Whisk in tarragon-flavored mustard, cream, and 2 tablespoons of chopped tarragon over medium heat. Allow to cook until sauce thickens. Thin with water, if necessary, at serving time. Carve chicken and serve hot with sauce. Garnish with additional tarragon sprigs.

Reci Tip—In order for the skin of a chicken to be crusty after roasting, brush the chicken with one or two spoonfuls of oil in addition to any butter you use.

Champagne Chicken
Poulet au Champagne

Très Simple

Preparation: 25 minutes
Cooking: 70 minutes
Servings: 4
Equipment: 6-quart ovenproof
    baking dish, 12-inch skillet

INGREDIENTS

1 3–4-pound chicken, trussed
3 tablespoons unsalted butter,
    divided use
4 onions (about 2 pounds),
    chopped
1 bay leaf
1 teaspoon fresh thyme, chopped
½ bottle champagne
1 pound mushrooms
1 cup whipping or light cream
2 teaspoons arrowroot (if using
    light cream)
¼ cup tarragon or truffles,
    chopped
Salt to taste
Freshly ground pepper to taste

This is a superb way to present chicken. Serve the rest of the champagne with the chicken. If truffles or tarragon are unavailable, any other fresh herb would be suitable. If using light cream, mix 2 teaspoons of arrowroot diluted in 1 tablespoon of water into the sauce to thicken it.

Preheat oven to 375°. Brown chicken in 2 tablespoons butter in a skillet over medium high heat for about 15 minutes. Remove chicken to a platter. Brown onions with bay leaf and thyme, stirring occasionally. Place chicken and onion mixture in baking dish and sprinkle with the champagne. Place in the oven and bake for 1 hour, uncovered.

Wash mushrooms in water with lemon juice or vinegar. Drain, dry, and slice. Melt remaining tablespoon of butter in a skillet and sauté mushrooms over medium heat for 10 minutes.

Set aside cooked chicken and mushrooms and keep warm on a serving platter. Skim fat from the pan juices. Add whipping cream to the pan juices and reduce until smooth. Alternately, place the juices and light cream in a saucepan over medium heat. Stir in diluted arrowroot and cook until thickened.

Season sauce with tarragon or truffles at the last moment. Add salt and pepper, if necessary. Pour sauce over the carved chicken and serve.

Reci Tip—When you open a bottle of champagne, put the handle of a silver spoon in it. The next day, the champagne will still be bubbly.

Chicken for a Winter Sunday
Poule-au-Pot d'un Dimanche Hivernal

Très Simple

Preparation: 15 minutes
Cooking: 4 hours
Servings: 6
Equipment: 8- to 10-quart stock-
    pot, 3-quart saucepan, strainer,
    whisk

INGREDIENTS

1 6-pound stewing chicken
3 carrots, peeled and sliced
1 large onion, peeled and sliced
Salt to taste
Freshly ground pepper to taste
2 round slices veal knuckle bones
3 leeks, trimmed
1 leafy rib celery, cleaned
1 sprig thyme
1 bay leaf
4 sprigs parsley

Preparation: 20 minutes

INGREDIENTS

5 tablespoons unsalted butter
7 tablespoons flour
4½ cups strained chicken stock
    from stewing chicken
2 egg yolks
Juice of 1 lemon

Yield: 3½ cups

Although this dish is delicious in winter, it can be served during any season, so don't save this recipe exclusively for the cold winter months. It provides a perfect family dinner for a Sunday gathering when everyone gets together to share conversation and ideas. A hen or stewing chicken makes a flavorful broth.

Place 3 quarts cold water in a stockpot. Add chicken, carrots, onion, salt, pepper, veal knuckles, leeks, and celery. Bring slowly to a boil, removing any surface foam that accumulates.

Reduce heat and simmer for 3½ hours with lid slightly ajar. After 50 minutes skim off any more fat or foam on the surface. Add thyme, bay leaf, parsley, salt, and pepper to taste.

The cooked chicken can be carved and served with its stock and vegetables in deep plates. Or it may be drained, carved, and served with Creamy Chicken Sauce, accompanied by rice.

This chicken stock is delicious served alone, garnished with croutons (p. 31), or store leftover stock in the refrigerator for later use.

Creamy Chicken Sauce

Reduce stock by 1 cup over medium heat. Melt unsalted butter in a saucepan. Mix in flour with a wooden spoon. Cook 1–2 minutes. Add hot, strained stock, whisking until smooth. Beat egg yolks with a little of the hot sauce to temper, then whisk yolks into the sauce in the pan. Add lemon juice and check seasoning. Do not boil again.

Chicken with Lemons
Poulet au Citron

Preparation: 15 minutes, plus 24
    hours to marinate
Cooking: 40 minutes
Servings: 4
Equipment: 1-gallon glass or
    plastic airtight container with
    lid, 1-quart saucepan, baking
    pan with rack

INGREDIENTS

1 chicken (about 3½ pounds)
⅓ cup onion, peeled and chopped
1 small bell pepper, seeded and
    cut in strips
2 cloves garlic, minced
¼ cup plus 2 tablespoons extra
    virgin olive oil, divided use
1 cup fresh lemon juice (from
    approximately 8 lemons)
1 bouquet garni (parsley, thyme,
    and bay leaf tied together)
Salt to taste
Freshly ground pepper to taste
2 teaspoons sugar
2 lemons for garnish
Fresh tarragon, mint, or parsley
    for garnish

Fragrant with its citrus flavor, this dish is ideally refreshing during the spring and summer. Add more sugar, if desired, to sweeten the tartness. Chicken with Lemons is an easy summer entrée that can be doubled for a gathering. Use colorful peppers for added visual impact.

The night before, cut chicken into 6 pieces. In an airtight container, combine onion, bell pepper, garlic, and chicken. Add ¼ cup olive oil and freshly squeezed lemon juice, and season with salt and pepper. Top with bouquet garni. Turn the chicken pieces once or twice while they are marinating overnight in the refrigerator.

The next day, preheat oven to 400°.

Remove chicken from the marinade, reserving marinade. Drain and place on a rack in an ovenproof baking pan. Brush chicken with the remaining 2 tablespoons of olive oil. Season with salt and pepper. Bake chicken for 40 minutes. If chicken is not as brown as you like, broil for a few minutes.

Cook marinade in a saucepan, covered, over low heat for 40 minutes. Add sugar while the marinade is cooking, stirring from time to time.

After chicken has cooked for 15 minutes, drain the liquid that has accumulated on the bottom of the pan and add to the saucepan with the marinade.

To serve, arrange cooked chicken on a serving platter. Removing bouquet garni, pour marinade over the chicken. Garnish with lemon slices and fresh herbs. Serve hot or at room temperature.

Quail with Red Bell Peppers
Cailles aux Poivrons Rouges

Preparation 15 minutes
Cooking: 2 hours
Servings: 6
Equipment: 12-inch skillet, high-sided baking dish just the size of the peppers

INGREDIENTS

6 quail (about 4 ounces each), cleaned
6 thin slices bacon
Salt to taste
Freshly ground pepper to taste
4 tablespoons unsalted butter, divided use
6 very large plump red bell peppers with flat bottoms
6 sprigs fresh thyme or 1 teaspoon dried
Butter for baking dish

Quail with Red Bell Peppers is an ideal dish for those who have a hunter in the family, although quail are readily available in most markets. A special pleasure of this dish is the little pool of delicious juice that forms in the bottom of each pepper. Different colored peppers make for a pretty presen tation, and the recipe can easily be increased.

Wash quail and pat dry. Insert a slice of bacon in each, salt and pepper, and brown lightly in a skillet with 2 tablespoons butter.

Preheat oven to 325°.

Cut the top off each bell pepper at the stalk end. Clean, and discard seeds. Place a quail inside each bell pepper, together with a sprig of thyme. It will be necessary to bend quail legs, keeping breast and neck side up when fitting into pepper.

Place filled peppers side by side in an ovenproof, high-sided, buttered baking dish. Place 1 teaspoon of butter on top of each and season with salt and pepper. Bake for 1½ hours, uncovered, basting bell peppers frequently with their juice.

Serve in the baking dish.

Reci Tip—Wild game, such as ducks or quail, are easier to pick clean if first dipped in paraffin. When the paraffin cools, pull off the paraffin and the feathers will be removed as well.

Pheasant in a Pot
Faisan en Cocotte

Très Simple

Preparation: 10 minutes
Cooking: 1 hour
Servings: 2
Equipment: heavy saucepan,
    8-inch skillet

INGREDIENTS

1 pheasant (about 3 pounds)
3 tablespoons unsalted butter,
    divided use
Salt to taste
12 small onions, boiling type
12 mushrooms
⅓ cup Madeira wine, Sercial
    (dry) or Malmsey (sweet)
Freshly ground white pepper to
    taste

The beautiful Château D'Ussé has always been known as the Sleeping Beauty château. In recent years past, the Marquis and Marquise always lived exactly like noble couples did back in the nineteenth century. Every night for dinner, they were served by a maître d' wearing white gloves. The Marquis wore a black tuxedo, the Marquise dined in a long gown, and their table was set with china and silverware, even if the meal only consisted of an omelette. Their grandsons were expected to wear tuxedos as well. But one night the grandsons created a "revolution" when they came to dinner in jeans. For the Marquis and Marquise, it was as though the world had ended. In reality, the Château D'Ussé had just entered the twentieth century a little later than the rest of us.

Have supplier clean and truss pheasant. Brown pheasant in 2 tablespoons of butter in a saucepan. When golden brown on both sides, sprinkle with salt, cover pan, and allow to cook gently for 15 minutes.

Peel onions. In a skillet, melt the remaining tablespoon of butter and brown onions. Clean and trim mushrooms, and wash them well. Place onions and raw mushrooms around pheasant in the casserole.

Add Madeira wine, cover casserole, and allow to finish cooking, 30–40 minutes. Pheasant is fully cooked if juices run clear when pricked near the top of the thigh. Check seasonings, adding freshly ground white pepper to taste. Serve accompanied by Celery Root Purée (p. 100) and a green salad.

—*Marquise de Blacas, Château d'Ussé*

Reci Tip—To keep an onion from falling apart, pierce it with a fork before cooking.

Stuffed Family-Style Veal Scallop
Escalope Familiale Farcie

Preparation: 45 minutes
Cooking: 1½ hours
Servings: 6
Equipment: kitchen string,
   12-inch skillet, meat pounder,
   heavy shallow pan with tight-
   fitting lid, size to hold veal

INGREDIENTS

1 slice of veal (1½ pounds) cut ⅜
   inch thick from veal rump or
   round
6 eggs
3 tablespoons fines herbes
   (parsley, chives, chervil, and
   tarragon), divided use
Salt to taste
Freshly ground pepper to taste
3 tablespoons unsalted butter,
   divided use
2 large slices cooked ham (about
   ⅓ pound) cut to fit over veal
10 ounces bulk breakfast
   sausage
2 shallots, minced
1 tablespoon cognac (optional)
2 medium onions, peeled and
   chopped
2 tablespoons hot water
2 cloves garlic
4 sprigs thyme
1 sprig rosemary
Additional thyme and rosemary
   sprigs for garnish

Even your most discriminating guests will be impressed when you bring Stuffed Family-Style Veal Scallop to the table. Ratatouille (p. 101) and Zucchini Flan (p. 106) make excellent accompaniments. If it is difficult to obtain a single large veal scallop, have the butcher pound two large veal scallops together. The grain of the meat should run lengthwise so the roll can be sliced across the grain.

Lay veal scallop on a board. Flatten with a meat pounder so that the scallop is a uniform thickness.

Beat eggs with a fork in a bowl, adding 2 tablespoons of fines herbes, salt, and pepper. Cook eggs like an omelette in 1 tablespoon of butter in a skillet, flipping once. Place cooked omelette on veal scallop and cover omelette with ham slices.

Break up sausage and season with shallots and 1 tablespoon fines herbes. Mix well and add cognac. Place on top of ham, smoothing over to flatten. Roll up the veal and fillings lengthwise, being careful to enclose all the stuffing. Tie roll with kitchen string at 1-inch intervals.

In a large, heavy pan melt remaining 2 tablespoons of butter and slowly brown veal rolls over medium heat, about 15 minutes. Add onions and stir for 1 minute. Add 2 tablespoons hot water, salt, pepper, garlic, thyme, and rosemary. Cover and allow to cook slowly on stove for 1 hour, turning meat from time to time. When finished cooking, remove from heat, cover loosely with foil, and set aside for 10 minutes before slicing.

The scallop may be served hot or cold with pan juices. Garnish with thyme and rosemary sprigs.

Agnes Sorel Veal Delights
Delices Agnes Sorel

Preparation: 30 minutes
Cooking: 30 minutes, plus
 35 minutes for sauce
Servings: 4
Equipment: blender or food
 processor, 4 6-ounce molds,
 8-inch skillet, 9-inch baking
 pan, 2-quart saucepan

INGREDIENTS

1 pound ground veal
2 eggs
3 tablespoons Béchamel Sauce
 (p. 91)
Salt to taste
Freshly ground white pepper to
 taste
3 tablespoons Sauce Périgueux
 Madère
¼ cup minced tarragon
3 tablespoons unsalted butter,
 divided use
6 mushrooms (4 ounces)
⅓ cup chopped ham (about 3
 ounces)
Tarragon, chives, or parsley for
 garnish

These delightful, delicious molds can be used for entertaining as well as for family dinners. The original recipe included truffles in the meat mixture as well as the sauce. If you have access to truffles, by all means use them. If not, the herbs add a lot of flavor by themselves. You may substitute ground chicken breast for the veal. The sauce is a wonderful addition to any roast meat or poultry.

Cover Béchamel Sauce with plastic wrap until use. Prepare the Sauce Périgueux Madère (facing page) and reserve.

Place ground chicken or veal in a food processor, blender, or bowl and add eggs, one at a time, beating well after each addition. Add Béchamel Sauce, salt, pepper, and minced fresh herbs, mixing well. Butter molds and fill with the mixture. Make a depression in the center of the mixture with your index finger dipped in water. Set molds aside.

Preheat oven to 400°.

Clean, trim, and chop mushrooms. Sauté mushrooms in skillet over medium heat in 1 tablespoon of butter until they have wilted and look dry. Remove from heat and stir in chopped ham; flavor with 3 tablespoons of the Périgueux sauce. Divide mixture equally and place in depression in center of molds. Place molds in a bain-marie and bake for 20 minutes covered loosely with aluminum foil. —*Château de Montpoupon*

½ cup minced carrot

½ cup onion, peeled and minced

1 shallot, peeled and minced

5 tablespoons unsalted butter, divided use

3 tablespoons flour, divided use

2 cups Meat Stock (p. 89)

⅓ cup Sercial Madeira wine

Salt to taste

Freshly ground white pepper to taste

Truffle peels (optional)

Yield: 1½ cups

Sauce Périgueux Madère

Melt 3 tablespoons butter in a saucepan. Add minced vegetables and cook over low heat until softened, about 10 minutes. Sprinkle with 1 tablespoon flour and mix well. Slowly add Meat Stock, whisking over medium heat until sauce begins to thicken, and cook 10 minutes. Strain sauce, discarding vegetables, into a clean saucepan. Add Madeira wine and simmer for 10 minutes. Combine 2 tablespoons flour and 2 tablespoons butter in a bowl and work into a paste. Whisk this mixture into sauce to thicken it, while sauce simmers an additional 5 minutes. Stir in truffles, if using, and season with salt and pepper.

Reci Tip—Decorating your table with living things makes dining come alive. You can usually find resources to enhance your table—flowers, greenery, and fruit—in your own backyard.

Veal Filet Mignon
Mignon de Veau à la Salomon

Preparation: 20 minutes
Cooking: 20–25 minutes
Servings: 2
Equipment: 12-inch skillet,
  whisk

Ingredients

4 small carrots, peeled
4 small turnips, peeled
1 rib celery, peeled
4 scallions
6 asparagus tips
½ cup fresh lima beans
1 artichoke
Juice of 1 lemon
1 whole veal filet mignon (about
  14 ounces)
1 tablespoon unsalted butter
1 cup dry white Touraine wine
  or Sauvignon Blanc
Salt to taste
Freshly ground pepper to taste
½ cup heavy cream
2 egg yolks
1 tablespoon chervil, chopped,
  for garnish

This recipe's name may be somewhat facetious, but it is also very accurate. Mignon de Veau à la Salomon was created for two servings only, and it has to be divided with the wisdom and judgment of Solomon. Humor aside, the recipe provides an elegant and special dinner for two. Or you can easily double the ingredients if you have another two guests. But it may be wise to let them play Solomon and divide their own servings.

Cut carrots, turnips, and celery into regular uniform "shoe-string" shapes or matchsticks. Wash and trim scallions. Remove tough ends of asparagus and shell lima beans, if necessary. Set aside.

Remove artichoke leaves and choke, retaining only the bottom. Cut into 4 wedges. Blanch 5 minutes in boiling, salted water to which lemon juice has been added. Drain and set aside.

Brown filet mignon slowly in butter in a heavy skillet over medium heat. Remove fat from pan and discard.

Add the vegetables to the veal. Pour in white wine until vegetables are half-covered. Add water if necessary. Cover and cook 15–20 minutes over medium low heat, until vegetables are tender. Remove vegetables and meat to a platter and keep warm. Taste liquid and season with salt and pepper. Whisk cream and egg yolks in a bowl. Add ¼ cup hot liquid from skillet to the yolks, whisking until combined. Return mixture to skillet, whisking until thick; do not boil.

Check seasoning. Slice veal judiciously and cover with sauce. Sprinkle with chopped chervil and serve hot.

—*Comtesse de Bouillé, Château des Réaux*

Beef in Shallot Sauce
Tournedos en Sauce Echalote

Preparation: 5 minutes
Cooking: 15–25 minutes
Servings: 2
Equipment: 8-inch sauté pan,
 fine strainer, whisk, 1-quart
 saucepan

Ingredients

2 tablespoons canola oil
4 tablespoons unsalted butter,
 divided use
2 beef mignon filets or boneless
 sirloin steaks, 8 ounces each
Salt to taste
Freshly ground pepper to taste
1 tablespoon minced shallot
5 tablespoons red Bordeaux
 wine
7 tablespoons Meat Stock,
 (p. 89)
1 teaspoon flour (optional)
1 tablespoon parsley, chopped,
 for garnish

This classic dish is better if you have the time to create your own meat stock from scratch. However, if you don't, substitute frozen stock or bouillon mixed with water, although you may have to adjust the salt if you use the latter. This dish will still be something that you will be proud to serve your family and guests.

Heat oil and 2 tablespoons butter in a sauté pan over medium high heat. Brown meat on both sides (rare, medium, or well-done, according to taste), season with salt and pepper, and set aside on a heated platter. Gently cook minced shallot in pan juices until soft.

Add red Bordeaux wine to sauté pan and deglaze the pan over medium heat by stirring to loosen the solids that flavor the sauce. Simmer and reduce liquid to half. Add Meat Stock and repeat the operation, reducing the liquid to half. Strain sauce through a fine strainer into a saucepan, pressing on the solids to extract the juice. Discard the solids.

Mix 2 tablespoons butter and flour; add to the pan, stirring constantly. Allow to cook and thicken. If not using flour, remove pan from the heat and whisk in the unsalted butter. Coat meat with hot sauce. Garnish with parsley.

For a party, cook a 3-pound whole tenderloin at 450° for 35 minutes. Increase quantities to 2 tablespoons shallots, 1¼ cups wine and ¾ cup Meat Stock. Cook as above. Diced marrow, as well as ½ cup cream, may be added to enrich the sauce. (Marrow is the center portion of beef or veal shank bones.)

Pot-au-Feu

Très Simple

Preparation: 25 minutes
Cooking: 4 hours
Servings: 4
Equipment: 10-quart stock pot
with cover, kitchen string,
strainer

INGREDIENTS

2 pounds fresh beef bones,
including one good marrow
bone, cut into pieces
3½ quarts cold water
3 pounds of beef rump, sirloin
tip, chuck or brisket roast
4 carrots (8 ounces), peeled and
chopped
4 leeks, green tops
discarded (8 ounces)
2 turnips (8 ounces), peeled and
chopped
4 ribs celery
1 bunch spring onions
2 teaspoons salt or to taste
Freshly ground pepper to taste
Cornichon pickles or sour
gherkins

The classic blending of beef and vegetables in Pot-au-Feu is
renowned as the national French dish. Although the
marrow bone is optional, your broth will certainly have more
flavor and body if you use it. The bonus, of course, is the
marrow, extracted with a small spoon and spread on thick slices
of toast, preferably sourdough rye. Be sure to serve coarse-
grained mustard, coarse sea salt, cornichon pickles, and steamed
potatoes as accompaniments. The broth is very flavorful, so save
the leftovers for use in soups and sauces.

Wash bones well and bring to a boil in 3½ quarts of salted water
in a deep, large pot. Skim off foam that rises to the surface for
about 10 minutes after water boils. (Several drops of cold water
thrown in boiling liquid helps skimming process.)

Lower flame so that liquid barely simmers. Add the beef. Skim
off any additional foam. Partially cover pot and simmer for 3
hours.

Cut vegetables into large pieces and tie them with kitchen string
in 3 or 4 bundles to make it easy to retrieve them later. Add vegetables to the meat after about 3½ hours, and cook additionally
for 30–40 minutes, until tender.

When beef is tender, remove from stock and cover loosely with
foil. Degrease and strain the stock. Season with salt and pepper
to taste.

Thickly slice beef and arrange on a platter, moisten with a little
stock and surround with vegetables and pickles. Serve stock in
cups as a soup.

Braised Beef
Boeuf Braisé

Très Simple

Preparation: 20 minutes
Cooking: 1½–3 hours
Servings: 6
Equipment: covered 4- to 6-
  quart casserole, tongs, strainer

INGREDIENTS

3–4 pound piece boneless beef,
  tied with string if necessary
  (choice of filet mignon, sirloin,
  rib roast, flank, chuck, or
  round roast)
2 pounds beef bones, cut into
  pieces by the butcher
2 tablespoons unsalted butter
2 ounces salt pork, diced
2 tablespoons cognac
3 tablespoons dry white wine
1 bouquet garni (thyme, parsley,
  and bay leaf tied together)
1 teaspoon salt
Freshly ground white pepper to
  taste

INGREDIENTS

1 pound mushrooms
6 tablespoons unsalted butter or
  pan drippings
¾ cup whole black olives, pitted

The preparation of Braised Beef, an easy party dish, requires an interesting technique that causes the meat to taste roasted even though it is actually braised, maintaining its juiciness. The bones add a lot of flavor to the tasty sauce, and a boneless rib roast will certainly please beef eaters. This braised dish may be served with Mushroom and Olive Garnish.

Brown meat and bones over medium heat in unsalted butter in a large, deep casserole. Push browned bones aside and brown salt pork in the same pan. Add cognac, white wine, bouquet garni, salt, and pepper. Cook slowly, covered, turning meat occasionally. More tender cuts of meat will take less time to cook: a rib roast about 1½ hours, a chuck roast 3 hours.

Remove cooked roast from pan. Remove string and, if necessary, pour off fat. Simmer pan juices, uncovered, until reduced to about 1 cup of liquid, about 15 minutes. Cover roast loosely with foil until serving.

Mushroom and Olive Garnish

Wash mushrooms in water containing some vinegar; drain and cut in thick slices. Cook them in butter or roast drippings. When browned, add to the beef sauce and heat, preferably 15 minutes before serving. You can also add washed, pitted, and dried olives (calamata, black, or niçoise) about 6 minutes after the mushrooms. Serve in a hot, deep dish.

Pork Roast with Oranges
Porc à l'Orange

Très Simple

Preparation: 10 minutes
Cooking: 1½ hours
Servings: 5
Equipment: 3-quart casserole
  with tight-fitting lid

INGREDIENTS

2 pounds boneless pork roast
2 tablespoons unsalted butter
3 medium onions, cut in rings
3 oranges, sliced (reserve 3 slices
  for garnish)
1 cup water or stock
1 cup tomato sauce or tomato
  purée
2 sprigs of fresh thyme or ½
  teaspoon dried
1 bay leaf
1 teaspoon granulated sugar
Salt to taste
Freshly ground white pepper to
  taste
1 tablespoon unsalted butter
1 tablespoon flour
Green leaves, such as kale or
  savoy, for garnish
Additional thyme sprigs for
  garnish

A boneless loin roast works well, but ask the butcher to tie it so the roast retains its shape. Pork Roast with Oranges can be served with Zucchini Salad with Mushrooms (p. 48) and White Onion Purée (p. 100) for a festive repast.

Brown pork roast over medium heat in unsalted butter in a large casserole. In the same pan, brown onions and sliced oranges. Add water or stock and tomato sauce or purée to the pan. Add thyme, bay leaf, sugar, salt, and pepper.

Cook, covered, over low heat for 1 hour or until roast's temperature is 170°. Check periodically, adding water or stock if dry. Turn roast several times during cooking.

Remove cooked roast to a platter and cover loosely with foil. If sauce is too thin, add, in small pieces, 1 tablespoon of butter and 1 tablespoon of flour, kneaded together, until desired consistency is obtained. Cook for a few more minutes, stirring constantly with a wooden spoon.

To serve, slice pork roast and arrange slices on a hot serving tray. Pour a little of the sauce over the roast. Garnish the edge of the platter with half slices of oranges, poached 1 minute in the sauce, and some green leaves and fresh thyme sprigs. Pour remainder of sauce in a gravy boat and serve with the meat.

Reci Tip—To keep a pork roast from shrinking during cooking, dip it in boiling hot water for a few seconds before cooking. —Laeticia de Germiny

Top: Fan-Shaped Eggplant (p. 95); bottom: Vegetables Gratin (p. 98)

*Red Bell Pepper Bavarois (p. 60), served with red
and yellow Extra Virgin Tomato Sauces (p. 90)*

Provençal Tomatoes (p. 102)

Potatoes au Gratin (p. 103)

Pork Roast with Oranges (p. 78)

Top: Veal Filet Mignon (p. 74); bottom: Braised Beef (p. 77)

Stuffed Family-Style Veal Scallop (p. 71) with Ratatouille (p. 101)

Lamb Stew with Fresh Spring Vegetables (p. 79)

Pot-au-Feu (p. 76)

Pheasant in a Pot (p. 70)

Lamb Stew with Fresh Spring Vegetables
Navarin aux Petits Légumes Nouveaux

Preparation: 20 minutes
Cooking: 1½ hours
Servings: 6
Equipment: fine strainer, 6-quart
casserole, 2½-quart saucepan

INGREDIENTS

1½ pounds lamb shanks, sliced ½
inch thick
1½ pounds boneless lamb
shoulder or lamb leg, cut in
medium cubes
2 tablespoons extra virgin olive
oil
2 tablespoons unsalted butter
1 teaspoon granulated sugar
1 tablespoon flour
4 large tomatoes, chopped
Salt to taste
Freshly ground white pepper to
taste
1 bouquet garni (parsley, thyme,
and bay leaf, tied together)
3 cloves garlic
1 bunch small new carrots
1 bunch small new turnips
1 bunch small new onions
1 pound peas (shelled)
¾ pound fresh green beans
1 teaspoon unsalted butter

For a beautiful presentation, prepare the fresh spring vegetables separately when serving Lamb Stew. Arrange the meat
and part of the sauce on a serving dish, then top the stew itself
with the colorful vegetables and the remainder of the sauce. The
rich, concentrated sauce makes this stew delicious.

Dry the meat with a paper towel. In a large casserole brown
meat over medium heat in olive oil and unsalted butter. Sprinkle
sugar and flour over the meat, stir, then add tomatoes, salt,
pepper, bouquet garni, and crushed garlic. Allow to simmer
slowly, covered, for 1 hour and 15 minutes. Remove meat with a
slotted spoon and strain sauce through a fine strainer into a
bowl. Return meat and sauce to the pan.

Peel and trim vegetables; quarter as necessary. Add all of the
vegetables except green beans to the casserole with the meat;
allow to simmer for 15 minutes longer.* Cook green beans in
lightly salted boiling water for 15 minutes. Drain and reserve
until serving time.

In a deep serving dish surround meat with vegetables and keep
warm. Reduce sauce if necessary. Check seasoning in sauce and
pour over meat and vegetables. Garnish with green beans.

Reci Tip—spring and summer vegetables are best when cooked
in a little water that is slightly salted. Vegetables
will be crunchy without losing their taste.

---

* Alternately cook the vegetables quickly in boiling, salted water separately,
then plunge them into cold water to retain crispness and color. Drain and set
aside. Using this method, the vegetables will need reheating at serving time
by tossing them in a skillet with 1 teaspoon of butter.

Cassoulet

Preparation: 2 hours
Cooking: 5½–6 hours
Servings: 20–24
Equipment: 6-quart saucepan,
    baking pan with rack, 6-quart
    casserole, 8-quart ceramic
    casserole about 13 inches
    across, bowl

Cassoulet—satisfying, aromatic, and hearty—can be an extraordinary party dish, especially during winter. You can prepare it over several days so all that is left to do on party day is the final cooking. Serve with an assortment of breads and salads. Haricots lingots are available in specialty stores.

Cook beans in a large pot with bay leaves, pepper, 3 cloves of garlic, and enough stock to cover beans by 3 times. (Bouillon may also be used. Dilute 2 large cubes for every quart of water.) Slowly simmer for 1½ hours, adding more liquid if necessary. Beans should be just cooked, not mushy. Set aside. Preheat oven to 375°. Wash, dry, and season the ducks with salt, pepper, and thyme. Place them on a rack in a shallow pan and roast for 1½ hours. Skin and bone cooked meat and set aside. (Reserve each meat on a separate plate.)

Brown pork roast in 4 tablespoons goose fat or olive oil over high heat in a heavy, deep casserole. When brown, remove meat and keep warm. Add tomatoes, shallots, 4 cloves of garlic, and onions to the pan and cook until soft, stirring. Stir in ¼ cup parsley, 2½ cups of stock, tomato paste, wine, salt, and pepper. Return the pork roast to the pan, bring to a boil, reduce heat, cover, and simmer for 1 hour. Remove pork roast and cut into 1-inch cubes. Reserve sauce. Cut sausage into 1-inch cubes or ½-inch-thick triangles. Remove goose breast from fat and shred meat. Reduce oven to 325°.

Ingredients

3 pounds haricots lingots
  (French white beans) or navy
  beans
4–5 quarts of chicken or duck
  stock, divided use
3 bay leaves
Freshly ground pepper to taste
7 large garlic cloves, minced,
  divided use
2 ducklings (4–5 pounds each)
Salt to taste
3 tablespoons dried thyme
2½ pounds pork loin roast,
  boned and tied
¾ cup goose fat or olive oil
7 tomatoes, peeled, seeded, and
  chopped
3 large shallots, chopped
3 cups chopped onions
1¼ cup chopped parsley, divided
  use
2 tablespoons tomato paste
1 cup white wine
1½ pounds cooked garlic sausage
  or Keilbasa
1 can goose breast, fat reserved
2–3 cups fresh white bread
  crumbs

In a very large ceramic ovenproof casserole, layer meats, beans, and liquid as follows. Coat the bottom of the casserole with a large spoonful of tomato liquid and some sausage. Add ¼ of drained beans. Arrange ⅓ of each of the 4 meats on top of the beans. Sprinkle with salt, pepper, and thyme. Spoon on more tomato liquid. Repeat, ending with a layer of beans. Pour in remaining tomato liquid to barely cover beans. Reserve the extra to add as the Cassoulet cooks.

Combine crumbs and 1 cup parsley in a bowl. Spread them over the top of the beans. Drizzle ½ cup goose fat or olive oil over the top. Bake 1 hour at 325°; a crust should have formed. Break and push in the crust with a large spoon. It will brown again, leaving a crust intact for serving. Bake for a total of 3 hours. The crust may be broken again; be sure to finish with a nice brown crust on top, adding additional bread crumbs if necessary. If the liquid boils away, add more reserved broth. Let cool for 20 minutes before serving.

Aunt Alice's Pie

Pâté de Tante Alice

Preparation: 25 minutes, plus 24
    hours to marinate
Cooking: 50 minutes
Servings: 6
Equipment: glass or plastic air-
    tight container with lid, rolling
    pin, 9-inch springform pan,
    brush, cookie sheet

INGREDIENTS

¾ pound veal (boneless sirloin,
    leg or shank), chopped in ½-
    inch cubes
¾ pound pork, boneless, fat re-
    moved, chopped in ½-inch cubes
2¼ cups dry white wine
3 onions, peeled and sliced
¼ cup minced fresh tarragon
    (or 1 tablespoon dried)
¼ cup minced fresh chives
    (or 1 tablespoon dried)
¼ cup minced fresh parsley
    (or 1 tablespoon dried)
2 tablespoons flour
Salt to taste
Freshly ground white pepper to
    taste
1 pound Puff Pastry Dough
    (pp. 131–32)

EGG WASH

1 egg yolk, beaten
1 teaspoon milk

Aunt Alice's Pie is beautiful and tasty, ideal for family dinner
when you want something different. Try serving the Grenadine Onion Preserves (p. 96) and Salad with Bacon (p. 136)
with this.

The day before, place cubed meat in airtight container. Place
thin rings from onion on top of the meat and cover with white
wine. Season with salt and pepper. Cover and marinate 24 hours
in refrigerator.

Allow Puff Pastry Dough to come to room temperature, about
20 minutes. Then roll it on a floured surface to ⅛ inch thick.
Place dough in springform pan, smoothing it in place. Trim
excess, leaving a ½-inch overhang. Roll scraps of the dough into
a piece that will fit as a cover for the pie and set aside wrapped
in a damp towel.

Preheat oven to 450°. Thoroughly drain the meat mixture, discarding the marinade. Place meat on the dough in the pan.
Sprinkle with 2 tablespoons flour. Arrange the rest of the onions
and herbs on top and season with salt and pepper. Cover with
pastry. Brush edges of the pastry with water or some egg wash
and fold exterior pieces of dough over to seal the cover. Brush
entire surface with the egg wash, using a pastry brush. Make a
small hole in center of pastry cover to allow steam to escape.

Bake pie on a baking sheet for 10 minutes on the lower shelf of
the oven. Reduce temperature to 375° and bake for 40 minutes.
Turn oven off and leave pie in for 15 minutes longer. Crust
should be a deep golden brown. Remove from oven and allow to
sit for 20 minutes before serving.

Oysters in a Bowl
Cassolette d'Huitres à l'Impromptu

Preparation: 40 minutes
Cooking: 15 minutes
Servings: 8
Equipment: knife, slotted spoon,
    12-inch skillet, oyster shucking
    knife

INGREDIENTS

48 oysters
⅔ cup Vouvray wine or dry
    white wine
½ cup diced carrots
½ cup diced turnips
½ cup diced leeks
⅓ cup diced mushrooms
¾ cup diced celery root
1 shallot, chopped
½ cup chopped zucchini
½ cup heavy cream
½ cup unsalted butter, cut into
    pieces and chilled
Juice of 1 lemon
Salt to taste
Freshly ground white pepper to
    taste
1 lemon for garnish

Don't be surprised when you discover that there are more vegetables than sauce in this dish. Raphaël Guillot has a real talent for cooking delectable yet simple food at Château des Coudreaux on Lake Geneva near Evian. You will find his colorful Oysters in a Bowl has a distinct flavor that is both excellent and concentrated.

Remove oysters from shell, saving their juice. Heat white wine in a skillet to a simmer. Blanch oysters in the white wine 2–3 minutes. Remove them with a slotted spoon and drain. Add reserved, strained oyster juice to the pan with the wine.

Adjust heat to medium and cook until wine mixture is reduced by half, skimming surface of any foam. Add vegetables. Cook for 3 minutes longer. With a slotted spoon transfer vegetables to a dish and set aside.

Add cream to the wine reduction in the pan. Reduce slightly; whisk in unsalted butter. Do not allow to boil. Check seasoning, adding lemon juice, salt, and white pepper. Return vegetables and oysters to the sauce to reheat.

Serve hot in small bowls, 6 oysters per person. Garnish with a lemon wedge.
—Raphaël Guillot

Reci Tip—To rid shellfish of sand and grit, wash them well in very salty water.

Trout with Chives
Truite à la Ciboulette

Très Simple

Preparation: 15 minutes
Cooking: 35 minutes
Servings: 6
Equipment: 12-inch nonstick
  pan, sharp knife

INGREDIENTS

2 small carrots (about 4 ounces)
1 round piece celery root, 1 inch
  thick (about ½ pound)
6 medium mushrooms (about 6
  ounces)
2 tablespoons heavy cream
Salt to taste
Freshly ground white pepper to
  taste
3 tablespoons finely chopped
  chives
6 small trout (about ¾ pound
  each) cleaned
2–3 tablespoons unsalted butter
1 bunch fresh chives for garnish
Lemons for garnish

Although this recipe was originally designed for trout, any small fish will work just as well. Be sure to use a nonstick pan since the skin has a tendency to stick. For a light summer meal, try serving Trout with Chives with Fan-Shaped Eggplant (p. 95). The leftover celery root can be used in Celery Root Purée (p. 100) or Grand Duchess Salad (p. 50)

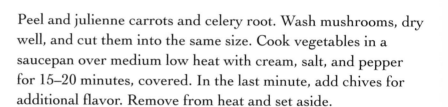

Peel and julienne carrots and celery root. Wash mushrooms, dry well, and cut them into the same size. Cook vegetables in a saucepan over medium low heat with cream, salt, and pepper for 15–20 minutes, covered. In the last minute, add chives for additional flavor. Remove from heat and set aside.

Wash and dry trout. Pepper the inside cavity and stuff it with no more than ⅙ of the mixed vegetables. Repeat for each fish. If there are any extra vegetables, serve them on the side with the fish.

Melt butter over medium high heat in a large skillet and sauté stuffed trout about 7½ minutes per side, turning once. Repeat for the remaining fish, wiping the skillet clean each time.

Arrange cooked trout on a hot serving platter. Garnish with fresh chives and lemon.
— *Château de Maintenon*

Reci Tip—To keep butter from spattering when sautéeing, salt the pan first.

Salmon in Parchment
Saumon en Papillote

Preparation: 20–30 minutes

Cooking: 10 minutes

Servings: 6

Equipment: foil or parchment
paper cut in 12-inch x 12-inch
squares, 13-inch x 18-inch
baking sheet

INGREDIENTS

6 filets fresh salmon (about 7
ounces each)

1 large tomato, peeled, seeded,
and diced

4 sorrel leaves, cut in chiffonade

3 large fresh mint leaves, snipped

Salt to taste

Freshly ground white pepper to
taste

6 teaspoons heavy cream or
white wine

The papillote method of cooking preserves the flavor and juice of the fish. You may easily substitute other fish and other herbs. Packets may be prepared in the morning and set aside in the refrigerator until dinner time. Cook as directed, allowing an additional 3–4 minutes. The steps of preparation might sound confusing, but with a little practice they are very easy. Serve with Celery Root Purée (p. 100).

Wash filets of salmon and pat dry.

Fold each foil or paper square in half and cut it to form a large heart shape.

Preheat oven to 425°. Place a filet of salmon on each heart to the right of center. On top of each filet place ⅙ of the tomato, sorrel, and mint. Season with salt, pepper, and a teaspoon of cream or wine. Fold foil or paper edges over. Starting with rounded edges of hearts, pleat and crimp edges of foil or paper to make an airtight seal, leaving fish loosely covered to form a tent in the center. Place packages on a baking sheet. Bake 10 minutes per inch of thickness of fish.

Serve packages on plates and allow your guests to be pleasantly surprised when cutting through the top of the package.

French Maxim—Two things that get better as they grow older are good wine and good friends.

Filet of Sole and Salmon Braised in Cream
Paupiettes de Sole et Saumon Braisées à la Crème

Très Simple

Preparation: 10 minutes
Cooking: 25 minutes
Servings: 8
Equipment: 12-inch skillet with
cover, meat pounder

INGREDIENTS

8 skinless sole filets (about 4
ounces each)
8 thin slices salmon (about 1½
ounces each)
¼ cup unsalted butter
1 shallot, chopped
6 ounces mushrooms (about 9
medium), julienned
1⅓ cups white wine
2 cups heavy cream
Juice of 2 lemons
Salt to taste
Freshly ground pepper to taste
Parsley or chives for garnish

When you buy your fish, try to get the sole filets all the same size. The salmon scallops should be cut like smoked salmon—scalloped on the diagonal—and about the same size as the sole. This can be served with steamed potatoes rolled in parsley or rice tossed with slivered vegetables.

Gently pound sole filets, if necessary, to flatten evenly. Place a scallop of salmon on each sole filet and roll up.

Melt butter in a sauté pan. Add chopped shallot and mushrooms. Sweat mixture over low heat, but do not brown. Cook until most of the liquid evaporates.

Place rolled fish on top of vegetables in the sauté pan. Add white wine, salt, and pepper. Cover and cook over medium heat for about 10 minutes. (If rolls are very thick, they will require longer cooking.) When cooked, remove filets with a slotted spoon and set them aside in a warm dish. Cover loosely.

Reduce cooking liquid by two-thirds over high heat. Add cream. Lower heat to medium and reduce by half. Season with salt, pepper, and lemon juice. Cover filets with sauce and serve hot. Garnish with parsley or chives. —*Raphaël Guillot*

Reci Tip—To keep herbs fresh, treat them like flowers. Cut the bottom of their stems and put them in water.
—The Vitry Family

Scallops on a Skewer
Brochettes de Coquilles Saint-Jacques

Preparation: 35 minutes
Cooking: 20 minutes
Servings: 4
Equipment: 1-quart bowl,
   12-inch ovenproof skillet, 4
   wooden skewers, baking pan
   large enough to hold skewers

INGREDIENTS

16 large sea scallops (about 1½
   pounds)
16 large shrimp, shelled and
   deveined
1 cup milk
2 red bell peppers, cut into 20
   pieces about 1 inch square
Salt to taste
Freshly ground white pepper to
   taste
Herbs from Provence (thyme,
   rosemary, and savory) to taste
3 tablespoons unsalted butter
¾ cup flour
3 tablespoons extra virgin olive oil

INGREDIENTS

¾ cup pitted whole black olives
2 ounces anchovies in oil, rinsed
   and dried
1 tablespoon paprika
4 tablespoons heavy cream
1 teaspoon capers
2 teaspoons fresh lemon juice

Yield: ⅔ cup

A delicious and unique entrée with a robust sauce. Serve on a bed of lightly steamed greens, such as spinach, along with French Pasta (p. 105) and Salad From Southern France (p. 44). When fresh rosemary is available on long stems, the sprigs can be stripped of their central leaves and used as skewers.

Rinse scallops and shrimp in cold water and pat dry. Soak scallops in milk for 20 minutes. Soak skewers in cold water for 30 minutes. Preheat oven to 350°.

Beginning with red pepper, place in order a piece of pepper, a shrimp, and a scallop on each skewer. Repeat, ending with a fifth piece of pepper. Season with salt and pepper and Herbs from Provence. Melt butter and olive oil in a pan large. Roll each skewer in flour, then sauté in the pan over medium high heat until browned all over. Place skillet in oven and bake 10 minutes.

To serve, arrange skewers on a platter and spoon some of the Olive-Anchovy Sauce on top. For a party, scoop out lemon halves and fill with the sauce. Garnish with fresh parsley.

Olive-Anchovy Sauce

Put olives and anchovies in an electric blender with paprika, heavy cream, capers, and lemon juice. Blend well. The sauce may be thinned with olive oil or more cream, if desired. Oil-cured olives will give a stronger flavor to the sauce. This sauce may also be used as a dip for vegetables or a topping for grilled fish or chicken.

Stocks and Sauces

INGREDIENTS

3 pounds chicken (or other
poultry) bones, including
necks and backs

4 quarts cold water

2 carrots, peeled and chopped

2 large onions, peeled and
chopped

2 ribs celery, chopped

1 bouquet garni (parsley, thyme,
and bay leaf tied together)

Salt to taste

Freshly ground pepper to taste

Yield: 2 quarts

Fresh homemade stocks result in the best flavors for your
sauces. However, there are bouillon substitutions for most
recipes. You can find ready-made stock in the frozen food sections of grocery stores and some specialty stores. And of course
canned and dried broth and bouillon are available in the soup
sections of supermarkets. Stocks may be kept in containers in
your freezer until they are needed.

Chicken Stock

Combine chicken parts and water in a large stockpot and slowly
bring to a boil. Skim surface as necessary for 15 minutes. Add
vegetables and bouquet garni. Lower heat and simmer for 4
hours, removing additional foam as necessary. When finished,
correct seasoning and strain through a fine strainer. Salt lightly
now or when used. Season with white or black pepper.

Cool stock in refrigerator. When fat has congealed on top,
remove and discard. Broth may be refrigerated for up to one
week or frozen for later use.

2 pounds veal and beef bones,
  cut into pieces

1 ham bone

1 piece bacon rind

4¾ quarts water

1 small turnip, chopped

2 carrots, peeled and chopped

2 large onions, peeled and
  chopped

2 sprigs parsley

1 sprig fresh thyme or ⅓ teaspoon dried

1 bay leaf

Yield: 2–3 quarts

Meat Stock or Bouillon

Combine bones, rind, and water in a large stockpot and slowly
bring to a boil. Skim surface as necessary for 15 minutes. Add
remaining ingredients and simmer gently for 4 hours. Cool
stock. Pour through a strainer. Salt and pepper as desired. Ham
bones in France are not all smoked as ours are. If you don't
want a smoky flavor, omit the ham and bacon and substitute
more beef and veal bones.

Concentrated Meat Stock

Reduce the finished stock by half. It will be solid when cold
because of the natural gelatin in the bones.

Bordeaux Wine Sauce
Sauce au Bordeaux

INGREDIENTS

2 tablespoons extra virgin olive
  oil
6 shallots, minced
Freshly ground pepper to taste
2 teaspoons flour
1 cup red wine, preferably a
  Bordeaux
1 sprig fresh thyme or ⅓
  teaspoon dried
1 bay leaf
Salt to taste

Yield: ¾ cup

This Bordeaux Wine Sauce is a classic red sauce that has been reworked in order to eliminate excessive butter. Light and tasty, it goes well with a variety of meats and fish.

Make this sauce in the same skillet in which you have been cooking beef, pork, or veal, or other dark meat. Drain fat from the skillet and heat the olive oil over medium heat. Add shallots and black pepper. Using a wooden spoon, stir shallots and scrape up the brown bits from the bottom of the skillet.

Stir in flour and cook for 30 seconds. Add red wine, thyme, and bay leaf, stirring until smooth. Reduce slowly to ¾ cup of liquid. Check seasoning, adding salt and pepper if needed. Serve with any cooked meat. —*Jean-Luc Debic, Chef, la Madeleine*

Extra Virgin Tomato Sauce

INGREDIENTS

1 tomato, red or yellow, 6–8
  ounces
¼ cup chicken broth (defatted)
1 tablespoon balsamic vinegar
1 tablespoon extra virgin olive
  oil
Salt to taste
Freshly ground pepper to taste
2 tablespoons fresh herb of
  choice, minced

Yield: 1 cup

Extra Virgin Tomato Sauce is perhaps the lightest and freshest, low-fat, all-purpose sauce you can make. You can drench steamed vegetables in it, serve it with Red Bell Pepper Bavarois (p. 60), or even dress a salad with the sauce.

Peel tomato, cut in half, and remove seeds. Place in a blender and purée. There should be about ½ cup of liquid or more. Add chicken broth, vinegar, oil, salt, and pepper with blender running. Pour sauce into a container, stir in the herbs, and set aside until serving time, refrigerating if more than 1 hour.

Fresh Tomato Sauce
Coulis de Tomates

INGREDIENTS

6–8 ripe tomatoes (about 2
  pounds)
4 tablespoons extra virgin olive
  oil
2 small onions, peeled and
  chopped
1 clove garlic, crushed
1 bouquet garni (parsley, thyme,
  and bay leaf tied together)
Salt to taste
Freshly ground pepper to taste
1 teaspoon sugar
Fresh herbs, such as basil,
  oregano, parsley, savory, or
  mint (optional)

Yield: 2 cups

You should plan on making large quantities of Fresh Tomato
Sauce when tomatoes are at their peak, then freeze the sauce
for use during winter when the vegetable gardens are bare.
Fresh herbs bring even more flavor to the recipe.

Peel tomatoes by dropping them into boiling water for one
minute, then placing tomatoes in cold water to cool. The peel
will slip right off. Cut into quarters and set aside. In a saucepan
heat olive oil, and add onion, garlic, and bouquet garni. Cook
over moderate heat, without browning, until the onions are soft.
Add the tomatoes. Bring mixture to a boil, reduce heat, and
allow to simmer until reduced by half, about 20 minutes. Add
salt, pepper, and sugar to taste.

Transfer the mixture to a blender and purée until fluid but thick.
Season with chopped fresh herbs. Cover sauce with ¼ inch of
olive oil if refrigerating several days, or freeze for future use.

Béchamel Sauce

INGREDIENTS

3 tablespoons unsalted butter
⅓ cup flour
2¼ cups milk, warmed
Salt to taste
Freshly ground white pepper to
  taste
Nutmeg to taste

Yield: 2½ cups

In a medium saucepan melt the butter over low heat. Whisk in
the flour. Mix well and cook for 2–3 minutes, stirring occasionally with a whisk.

Add warm milk, whisking constantly and cooking until the
sauce has thickened. Season with salt, pepper, and nutmeg. If
not using immediately, place plastic wrap on the surface or rub
with additional unsalted butter to keep a skin from forming.

VEGETABLES

Fan-Shaped Eggplant
Les Aubergines en Eventail

Grenadine Onion Preserves
Confiture d'Oignons à la Grenadine

Buttered Endives
Endives au Beurre

Vegetables Gratin
Gratin Méridional

Carrot Purée
Mousseline de Carottes

White Onion Purée
Purée d'Oignons Blancs

Ratatouille

Provençal Tomatoes
Tomates Provençales

Potatoes au Gratin
Gratin Dauphinois

Parisian Potatoes
Pommes de Terres Parisiennes

French Pasta
Pasta Française

Zucchini Flan with Garlic Cream
Flan de Courgettes à la Crème d'Ail

Fan-Shaped Eggplant
Les Aubergines en Eventail

Preparation: 20 minutes
Cooking: 30–45 minutes
Servings: 6
Equipment: 9-inch x 13-inch
   oven dish, or au gratin pan

INGREDIENTS

6 small eggplants, 8–12 ounces
   each
6 tomatoes
⅓ cup extra virgin olive oil
1 onion, peeled and chopped
1 clove garlic, minced
6 artichoke hearts, frozen or
   canned, sprinkled with lemon
   juice, cut into quarters
Several whole black Niçoise or
   Calamata olives, pitted
Salt to taste
Freshly ground pepper to taste
Fresh basil, oregano, or thyme to
   taste

As the warm afternoons of summer descended upon nineteenth century Provence, elegant ladies paraded gracefully in the town square, keeping themselves as cool as possible with their beautiful fans, called "éventails." This eggplant dish is reminiscent of the fans that captured the essence of a summer scene so long ago in Provence. This is a beautiful dish, and it should be served when the tomatoes are juicy and red.

Wash and trim eggplants. Cut them in half lengthwise. Place cut side face down and cut in 3 or 4 strips lengthwise, but do not detach the strips from stalk end. The result will be fan-shaped eggplant halves. Preheat oven to 350°.

Wash tomatoes, core, halve, and cut into ½-inch slices. Make sure tomatoes and eggplants are equal in height.

Lightly coat bottom of an oven dish with a thin layer of olive oil. Spread onions and garlic on top. Place fan-shaped eggplants in dish, flat side down, in close proximity to each other for support. Place slices of tomatoes between strips of fanned eggplants.

Place artichoke hearts and olives in the space between eggplant halves and sprinkle with ¼ cup olive oil. Season with salt and pepper to taste. Tuck herb stems or leaves among the vegetables.

Bake uncovered for 30–45 minutes, basting occasionally with pan juices. Serve hot as a vegetable or at room temperature as a first course, garnishing with more chopped herbs.

Grenadine Onion Preserves
Confiture d'Oignons à la Grenadine

Très Simple

Preparation: 15 minutes
Cooking: 60 minutes
Servings: 4–6
Equipment: 12- to 14-inch skillet
(or 6-quart pan), wooden
spoon

INGREDIENTS

½ cup unsalted butter
1½ pounds onions (about 5),
peeled and sliced thin
1½ teaspoons salt
1½ teaspoons freshly ground
pepper to taste
1⅓ cups sugar
1 cup sherry vinegar
1½ tablespoons Grenadine con-
centrate or Crème de Cassis
1⅔ cups Algerian or other red
wine

In the gardens of Provence, onions are taken from the ground with their long stems left intact, placed in the sun to dry, then artistically woven into braids and hung on kitchen walls. They are handy when it is time to create Grenadine Onion Preserves, a very pungent condiment whose strong flavors perform magic with smoked meats, game, or lamb.

Melt unsalted butter in a noncorrosive skillet. Continue cooking over medium heat until light brown, with a nutty aroma.

Add onions, salt, pepper, and sugar. Mix well with a spoon.

Cover skillet and cook for 30 minutes over low heat. Stir from time to time with a wooden spoon to prevent burning.

Add vinegar, Grenadine, and red wine. Cook gently, uncovered, 30 minutes longer, continuing to stir regularly with a spoon to prevent scorching or burning. Mixture will reduce and thicken. When cooked, cool and transfer to a jar or a bowl. You may remove the film of oil on the surface if you are serving the preserves cold, or simply stir it in if serving warm. The film acts as a preservative when you keep the mixture in the refrigerator.

—*Michel Guérard*

Reci Tip—Remember, after shaking the hand of a friend or guest, or handling a menu, the very last thing you should do before you touch either the foods you are preparing or about to eat is wash your hands. Follow this tip and you won't end up in bed with the flu.

Buttered Endives
Endives au Beurre

Très Simple

Preparation: 10 minutes
Cooking: 30 minutes
Servings: 6–8
Equipment: 12-inch to 14-inch
    casserole or skillet with cover

INGREDIENTS

2 pounds Belgian endives
6 tablespoons unsalted butter,
    divided use
Juice of 1 lemon
1½ cups water
Salt to taste
Freshly ground pepper to taste
Fresh tarragon, parsley, or
    chervil for garnish

Belgian endives, so popular in France, are found in the specialty produce sections of most grocery stores. The elongated, creamy white vegetables are also known as "witloof." The long shoots are cultivated in the stone caves of France, growing alongside mushrooms. The cool temperature and lack of light in the caves produce the distinctive paleness and flavor of this refined and delicious vegetable.

Clean endives carefully in water. Trim off the root end and drain. Dry well in a towel.

Place endives side by side in a pan with 2 tablespoons of unsalted butter, lemon juice, and water. Sprinkle with salt and pepper. Cover pan and bring to a boil; reduce heat and simmer gently for 20 minutes.

Pour contents of the pan into a colander and drain. Clean and dry the pan. In it melt the remaining 4 tablespoons of unsalted butter and return endives to heat slowly. Cook for 10 minutes, turning occasionally. Serve with a chopped fresh herb that complements the flavor of the main course. Season with salt and pepper, if needed.

Reci Tip—To give Belgian endives a good, light color and to rid them of bitterness, cook with the juice of a lemon and 2 teaspoons of sugar.

Vegetables Gratin
Gratin Méridional

Très Simple

Preparation: 15 minutes
Cooking: 60–90 minutes
Servings: 6
Equipment: 9-inch x 13-inch
   baking dish or au gratin dish

INGREDIENTS

5 tablespoons extra virgin olive
   oil, divided use
1 pound new potatoes, peeled
   and sliced
1 pound onions, peeled,
   trimmed, and sliced
1 pound zucchini, sliced
1 pound tomatoes, sliced
9 tablespoons Meat Stock (p. 89,
   or substitute 1 bouillon cube
   dissolved in ½ cup water or
   canned broth)
Salt to taste
Freshly ground pepper to taste
3 stems each parsley and rosemary, chopped, plus additional
   for garnish

For the most attractive presentation of this delicious and
healthful dish, try to buy vegetables of the same diameter.
Vegetables Gratin is a family favorite in the South of France,
one that is even better the next day. The dish is good served at
room temperature.

Grease baking dish with 1 tablespoon olive oil. Preheat oven to
400°.

Arrange vegetables overlapping in the following order: potatoes,
onions, zucchini, and tomatoes, making 2–3 layers.

Sprinkle 4 tablespoons of olive oil and the Meat Stock over vegetables. Season with salt, pepper, chopped parsley, and rosemary to taste.

Bake uncovered for 1–1½ hours, or until potatoes are tender.
Remove from oven and serve immediately, garnished with more
parsley.

Reci Tip—To keep parsley fresh, put it in a plastic bag in
         your refrigerator, but keep the bag open. Or, you
         can put the parsley upside down in a glass of
         water and place it in the refrigerator.
                                        —Danielle Renard

Carrot Purée
Mousseline de Carottes

Preparation: 25 minutes
Cooking: 40 minutes
Servings: 8–10
Equipment: 1½-quart saucepan,
    6-quart saucepan, food mill,
    whisk

INGREDIENTS

1¼ pounds potatoes, peeled and
    coarsely chopped
3 pounds carrots, peeled and
    sliced thick
3 tablespoons unsalted butter,
    divided use
1 medium onion, minced
⅔ cup heavy cream, heated
Pinch of sugar
2 egg yolks, beaten
Salt to taste
Freshly ground white pepper to
    taste

Carrots are used frequently in French country cooking, and this Carrot Purée is a colorful, elegant way to present them. A different, memorable way to serve the purée is to pipe it through a pastry bag into summer squash shells that have been blanched for 1 minute. The whole family will enjoy this year-round favorite.

Cook potatoes in salted water over medium heat until tender, about 30 minutes. Drain and dry them.

Blanch carrots in boiling, salted water for 10 minutes. Drain.

Melt 2 tablespoons of butter in a thick-bottomed saucepan. Add carrots and onions. Cover and allow to stew over low heat until carrots and onions are tender, but do not allow to burn or change color.

Pass all of the cooked vegetables through a food mill fitted with a fine disk, adding hot cream, spoonful by spoonful.

Return purée to pan over low heat. Stir in a pinch of sugar. Just before serving, add some of the hot purée to the egg yolks and remaining tablespoon of butter, to temper. Stir mixture into the remaining purée. Season to taste with salt and pepper. Serve hot. Keep warm in a bain-marie or double boiler, if necessary.

Reci Tip—You can tell how fresh an egg is by placing it in cold, salted water. If the egg sinks, the egg is fresh. If the egg floats on water, the egg is bad. Do not use it.

White Onion Purée
Purée d'Oignons Blancs

Très Simple

Preparation: 10 minutes
Cooking: 25 minutes
Servings: 4
Equipment: 2½-quart saucepan,
colander, blender, food mill,
whisk, bain-marie or double
boiler

Ingredients

1½ pounds onions, peeled and
quartered
1 pound potatoes, peeled and
quartered
⅔ cup heavy cream
Grated fresh nutmeg
Salt to taste
Freshly ground white pepper to
taste

Easy to make, White Onion Purée is excellent with any roasted meat or poultry. Vegetable purées are quite popular in France because they are light and healthy. So use your own unlimited imagination and create others, using any cooked vegetables or beans that might strike your fancy. Potatoes add richness and body to the recipe. Peel the onions under running water to avoid tears.

Boil salted water in saucepan and add onions and potatoes. Reduce heat and simmer 25 minutes, covered. Drain vegetables well in a colander and purée in a blender or pass through a food mill fitted with a fine disk. Add cream and nutmeg and beat with a whisk to a light purée. Season with salt and pepper to taste. Keep warm in bain-marie or double boiler if holding any length of time before serving.

Celery Root Purée

Substitute an equal weight of celery root for onions, cook for 5 minutes, then add potatoes. Proceed as above. Eliminate nutmeg, but enrich the purée with 3 tablespoons of butter added with the cream.

Turnip Purée

Substitute an equal weight of turnips for the onions and use only ½ pound of potatoes. Proceed as above. Eliminate nutmeg. Whip cream until thick before folding into the purée.

Ratatouille

Preparation: 30 minutes
Cooking: 1 hour
Servings: 4–6
Equipment: tall 6-quart
   casserole

INGREDIENTS

1 tablespoon extra virgin olive
   oil
1 large onion, peeled and diced
1 large clove garlic, minced
1 pound zucchini, sliced 1 inch
   thick
1 pound eggplant, peeled and
   sliced 1 inch thick
1 pound tomatoes, quartered
1 large green pepper, seeded and
   sliced
1 rib celery, uncut
1 small bunch fresh thyme
1 whole bay leaf
Salt to taste
Freshly ground pepper to taste
Fresh thyme for garnish
Fresh parsley, chopped, for
   garnish
Garlic, chopped, for garnish

Ratatouille became popular in Provence because the farmers spent so much of their time working in the fields. It was easy for them to throw vegetables into a pot and leave them to gently stew throughout the day. Ratatouille is a simple, rustic country dish that is reminiscent of a summer garden. If you prefer a finer texture, just dice all the vegetables. It is delicious as a main course over brown rice with grated cheese, as a filling for crèpes or omelettes, or as a vegetable side course.

Heat olive oil over medium heat in casserole. Add onion and cook over low heat for five minutes, then add garlic and cook for 2–5 minutes more, stirring often.

Add zucchini, eggplant, tomatoes, green pepper, celery, thyme, bay leaf, salt, and pepper. Mix well to combine ingredients. Cover casserole and bring to a boil. Reduce heat and let simmer, stirring occasionally, until juices are near top of vegetables, about 30 minutes. Remove lid and continue to cook for approximately 30 minutes, or until desired texture is reached. The mixture should be thick and the liquid should have evaporated.

Remove tomato skins, celery rib, and thyme; they should float to the top. Drain any excess liquid, if necessary. Pour into a serving dish and garnish with fresh thyme, parsley, and garlic, if desired.
                                    — *Terrie Warren, la Madeleine*

Reci Tip—To rid vegetables of those "unwanted little friends," put vinegar in the water when washing them.
                                    —The Vitry Family

Provençal Tomatoes
Tomates Provençales

Très Simple

Preparation: 40 minutes
Cooking: 20–30 minutes
Servings: 6
Equipment: food processor,
    11-inch x 13-inch baking pan

INGREDIENTS

6 fully ripe, juicy tomatoes about
    3 inches in diameter
Salt to taste
Freshly ground white pepper to
    taste
6 slices white bread
3 garlic cloves, minced
½ cup minced parsley
3–4 tablespoons extra virgin
    olive oil

The tomato has long been synonymous with Provence, where cooking is home-style, not the kind of cuisine that is generally found in a restaurant. The cook in Provence never uses an overabundance of ingredients in any one dish, always believing that the maximum amount of flavor is derived from the minimum amount of work.

Wash and dry tomatoes. Cut in half crosswise, seed, and season with salt and pepper. Place them face down in a deep dish for ½ hour to allow water to drain from tomatoes.

Preheat oven to 400°.

Process bread in a food processor or blender until it becomes crumbs. In a bowl mix bread crumbs with garlic and parsley.

Fill tomato halves with bread crumb mixture. Sprinkle a few drops of olive oil on each tomato half. Place them in an oiled baking dish side by side and bake for 20–30 minutes. Brown under a hot broiler to crisp the crumbs, if necessary. Serve hot.

Goat Cheese Tomatoes

Follow procedure above, but before filling tomatoes with bread crumbs, spread 1 ounce of soft goat cheese into each tomato half. Top with the crumbs and bake as above. Other herbs may be used, such as thyme or basil.

Potatoes au Gratin
Gratin Dauphinois

Preparation: 15 minutes
Cooking: 60–75 minutes
Servings: 4
Equipment: 2½-quart saucepan, au gratin pan, sharp knife or food processor, wooden spoon

INGREDIENTS

1 bay leaf
1 cup milk
4 tablespoons unsalted butter, divided use
Salt to taste
Freshly ground white pepper to taste
Grated fresh nutmeg to taste
1 cup heavy cream
1 pound potatoes, peeled and sliced very thin
1 clove garlic, peeled and cut in half
⅔ cup grated Gruyère cheese

When wheat crops failed in eighteenth-century France, an attempt was made to make the humble potato replace bread as a staple of the French peasants' diet. In time, the potato became the most popular vegetable in France. Potatoes au Gratin is uniquely French and different from American recipes. This recipe originated in the French Alps, where potatoes were cooked in earthenware pots on the hearth. The cheese melted and became golden brown; the dish was served piping hot, rich in both aroma and taste.

Boil milk with bay leaf in saucepan, taking care not to let it boil over. Preheat oven to 325°.

Add 3 tablespoons butter, salt, pepper, grated nutmeg, cream, and potatoes to the pan with the hot milk. Simmer, stirring from time to time with a wooden spoon to separate potatoes. Cook 20 minutes or until just tender. Remove from heat and set aside.

Grease an au gratin dish with remaining 1 tablespoon of butter. Rub dish with cut piece of garlic. Pour in potato mixture and sprinkle with grated Gruyère cheese.

Bake potatoes for 40–45 minutes. If surface of potato mixture is not browned sufficiently, place under broiler for about 3 minutes. Remove and let cool for 5 minutes before serving.

French Maxim—To invite people into your home is to take charge of their happiness during the time they are under your roof.

Parisian Potatoes
Pommes de Terres Parisiennes

Très Simple

Preparation: 15 minutes
Cooking: 30 minutes
Servings: 4
Equipment: 12-inch or 14-inch
  skillet, knife

INGREDIENTS

2 tablespoons unsalted butter
1 large onion, peeled and sliced
½ cup water
½ cup white wine
5 medium potatoes, peeled and
  cut into ½-inch cubes
Freshly ground pepper to taste
2 tablespoons chopped parsley
3 sprigs thyme
1 bay leaf
Salt to taste

There is something to be said for simplicity in cooking, and this recipe proves the point. Parisian Potatoes is a felicitous blend of flavors, very simple, very plain, and more importantly, very good.

Melt unsalted butter in large skillet. Add onions and cook until soft. Pour in water and wine, then add potatoes. Stir gently. Cook uncovered over low heat 10 minutes.

Add pepper, parsley, thyme, and bay leaf; continue cooking until liquid evaporates and potatoes are tender, about 20 minutes. Season with salt.

French Pasta

Pasta Française

Très Simple

Preparation: 10 minutes
Cooking: 12 minutes
Servings: 4
Equipment: 12-inch sauté pan,
   colander, 3- to 6-quart
   saucepan

INGREDIENTS

11 ounces dried spaghetti
2 tablespoons extra virgin olive
   oil
1 tablespoon minced garlic
1 teaspoon freshly ground black
   pepper
½ ounce chopped fresh parsley
¼ cup grated Parmesan Cheese
Salt to taste

Zesty with the flavor of garlic, yet tamed by the parsley, this is the flavorful pasta served at la Madeleine. As an entrée, this will serve two.

Cook pasta in boiling, salted water until just tender, about 10 minutes. Combine olive oil, garlic, and pepper in a sauté pan and cook gently until garlic is golden. Do not burn the garlic; if garlic looks like it is beginning to burn, remove from heat. Drain the cooked pasta in a colander and add to sauté pan. Toss gently; add parsley and toss again. Serve, topped with cheese. Season with salt, if desired.

—la Madeleine

King Henry II ate with his fingers. But then, so did everybody else in France until the king happened to stop by a popular inn, La Tour d'Argent, on a fateful night in 1552. Nearby he saw a table of Italians pull some sharp pointed instruments out of little cases and begin picking up meat without using their fingers at all.

King Henry knew a good idea when he saw one. He wiped the grease off his fingers and immediately introduced the fork to the royal court, calling it the greatest discovery of the century. His countrymen were not impressed, saying, "Why should we use forks and replace our hands, which were given by God?" God may have made fingers, but King Henry put a fork between them. —Claude Terrail, La Tour d'Argent

Zucchini Flan with Garlic Cream

Flan de Courgettes à la Crème d'Ail

Preparation: 20 minutes
Cooking: 30 minutes
Servings: 6
Equipment: 2½-quart saucepan,
   steamer, blender, pan for bain-
   marie, 3-cup mold for flan,
   1-quart saucepan

INGREDIENTS

1¾ pounds zucchini, chopped
4 eggs
½ cup plus 2 tablespoons heavy
   cream
Salt to taste
Freshly ground pepper to taste
½ teaspoon nutmeg
2 teaspoons unsalted butter
Spinach or lettuce and parsley
   for garnish

INGREDIENTS

3 cloves garlic, unpeeled
½ cup water
½ cup plus 2 tablespoons heavy
   cream
4 ounces unsalted butter, cold,
   cut in pieces
Juice of 2 lemons
Salt to taste

Yield: 1¼ cups

Garlic, grown in the fields of Brittany since the fifteenth century, has long been a staple of French country cooking. Garlic cream adds the perfect touch to the Zucchini Flan, whose contrasting colors of green and white can brighten any party, especially if you place the flan on lightly steamed spinach. The dish can be used as a first course or salad, as well as a vegetable.

Preheat oven to 400°. Steam zucchini for 20 minutes. Transfer zucchini to a blender or food processor and purée. Add eggs one at a time, blending after each addition. Pour in cream and season with salt, pepper, and nutmeg. Butter either small molds, a crown mold or a soufflé mold. Fill mold with the mixture and place in a bain-marie in the oven for 20–30 minutes. Check with a skewer or knife. A knife inserted will come out clean when flan is cooked.

Wash and drain lettuce or steam washed spinach. Unmold zucchini flan in center of platter. Garnish with either whole or chopped spinach or lettuce leaves. Decorate with sprigs of parsley. Surround with semi-warm Garlic Cream and serve.

Garlic Cream

Cook unpeeled garlic for 10 minutes in salted water. Peel and reduce garlic to a purée with a mortar and pestle or a fork. Place purée in a saucepan and add cream. Heat to boiling point; remove from heat and whisk in pieces of unsalted butter (or leave cream on heat and whisk in ¾ cup cold chicken broth mixed with 1 tablespoon arrowroot, and return to a boil to thicken). Whisk constantly to thicken sauce. Add lemon juice and season to taste with salt.

DESSERTS

Hazelnut Cake with Raspberry Sauce
Gâteau aux Noisettes au Coulis de Framboises

Apple Cake
Le Cake aux Pommes

Madeleine Cakes
Madeleines

Easy Chocolate Cake
Gâteau Facile au Chocolat

Chocolate Truffles
Truffes au Chocolat

Chocolate Marquise Royale
Marquise Royale au Chocolat

Almond Lace Cookies
Tuiles aux Amandes

Almond Tartlets with Fruit Preserves
Amandine à la Purée de Fruits

Raspberry Tart
Tarte aux Framboises

Apple or Pear Tart
Tarte aux Pommes ou aux Poires

Quick Apple Tart
Tarte Fine Minute aux Pommes

Madame Henriette's Tart
Tarte Madame Henriette

Emperor's Omelette
Kaiserschmarren

Lemon Soufflé
Soufflé au Citron

Pear Soufflé
Soufflé aux Poires

Pears Poached in Red Wine
Poires Pochées au Vin Rouge

Fruit Sherbet
Sorbet aux Fruits

Fresh Fruit Sauce
Coulis de Fruits Frais

Almond Cream
Crème d'Amandes

English Cream
Crème Anglaise

Almond Tart Dough
Pâte Sablée aux Amandes

Sweet Tart Dough
Pâte à Tarte Sucrée

Puff Pastry Dough
Pâte Feuilletée

Hazelnut Cake with Raspberry Sauce
Gâteau aux Noisettes au Coulis de Framboises

Preparation: 20 minutes
Cooking: 50 minutes
Servings: 8
Equipment: small roasting pan, towel, mixer, 8½- to 9-inch springform pan or 6-cup loaf pan, parchment paper

INGREDIENTS

1 cup hazelnuts, husked
4 egg yolks
1¼ cups sugar
⅔ cup oil
1 cup cake flour
5 egg whites, beaten stiff
Unsalted butter for pan
2 tablespoons powdered sugar for decoration

INGREDIENTS

½ pound fresh raspberries
Juice of 1 lemon
1¼ cups sugar

Yield: 2 cups

The timeless combination of hazelnuts and raspberries mingle to produce a wonderful dessert that is elegant, nutty, and rich. Decorate with extra berries during the summer.

Place hazelnuts in a preheated 400° oven for 5 minutes to roast. Rub nuts together, wrapped in a towel, to rid them of their skins. Mince finely with a knife or a food processor. Reduce oven to 350°.

Using a mixer, beat the egg yolks; add sugar and beat again. Add oil and mix, then flour, then nuts, and mix. Fold in egg whites. Add a small amount of the egg whites to lighten the batter before gently folding in remainder.

Place mixture in springform pan or loaf pan lined with buttered parchment paper. Bake about 40 minutes. Check the center with a toothpick to determine if mixture needs to bake longer. Toothpick should come out clean. Unmold and allow to cool. Sift 2 tablespoons powdered sugar over cake when completely cooled.

Raspberry Sauce

Purée raspberries with lemon juice and sugar in a blender or food processor for 3 minutes. Chill if desired. Serve surrounding cake or separately.

—*Raphaël Guillot*

Reci Tip—If you want to keep tarts and cakes moist and soft, simply put them in a box with a freshly washed whole apple.
—Danielle Renard

Apple Cake
Le Cake aux Pommes

Preparation: 25 minutes
Cooking: 60 minutes
Servings: 16–20
Equipment: two 9-inch round
    cake pans, mixer, brush

INGREDIENTS

1½ cups plus 2 tablespoons
    softened unsalted butter,
    divided use
2 tablespoons flour
2 cups sugar
8 eggs
3 tablespoons rum
½ cup buttermilk
4½ cups cake flour
½ cup powdered sugar
1 tablespoon baking powder
1 pound peeled and diced apples
    (or cherries or apricots)
Apricot preserves
½ cup roasted slivered almonds
    for garnish

The orchards of Calvados are thick with apple trees. More than a hundred varieties of apple trees cluster in the fields of a region where apple brandy was being enjoyed as early as 1533. Rémy Schaal, one of our original associates, is from Alsace. He can take those apples and create one of the finest cakes you can put on your table. The cake is never too sweet, has a dense crumbly texture, and is moist with apples. It is little wonder why the cake is so good. After all, Alsace is reputed to be the home of the best pastry chefs and bakers in all of France.

Preheat oven to 350°. Grease cake pans with 2 tablespoons of butter, then dust with flour and set aside.

Using a mixer, cream 1½ cups butter and sugar together. Add eggs one at a time, beating well after each addition. Add rum and buttermilk, mixing again. Sift together cake flour, powdered sugar, baking powder and add to above ingredients. Finally, fold in apples.

Spread cake into the two prepared cake pans. Bake for 60 minutes or until center is cooked.

Unmold cakes on a cloth. Remove pans. The cakes may be glazed with slightly melted apricot preserves and garnished with almonds.
—*Rémy Schaal, Head Chef, la Madeleine*

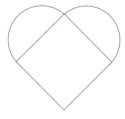

Reci Tip—Make a heart-shaped cake by using one square cake pan and one round cake pan of the same size. Lay square cake out in diamond formation. Cut round cake in half and place halves at the top of the square cake. —The Vitry Family

Madeleine Cakes
Madeleines

Très Simple

Preparation: 20 minutes
Cooking: 12 minutes
Yield: 24–36 madeleines
Equipment: madeleine molds,
   3-quart mixing bowl, wooden
   spoon

INGREDIENTS

4 eggs
1¼ cups plus 2 tablespoons sugar
1¼ cups plus 2 tablespoons flour
1½ teaspoons baking powder
Zest of 1 lemon
½ cup unsalted butter, melted

The great French novelist Marcel Proust wrote about madeleines in his book *Swann's Way:* "One day in winter on my return home, my mother, seeing that I was cold, offered me some tea, a thing I did not ordinarily take. . . . She sent for one of those squat, plump little cakes called 'petites madeleines,' which look as though they had been molded in the fluted valve of a scallop shell. . . . I raised to my lips a spoonful of the tea in which I had soaked a morsel of cake. No sooner had the warm liquid mixed with the crumbs touched my palate than a shudder ran through me. . . . An exquisite pleasure had invaded my senses." We hope your memories of madeleines are as happy as Proust's were.

Butter madeleine molds, sprinkle with flour, and shake to remove excess.

Mix eggs and sugar in a bowl, using a wooden spoon. When mixture is smooth, add flour mixed with baking powder, grated lemon zest, then the melted butter.

Fill each mold about half full and allow to stand 20 minutes. Preheat oven to 350°.

Bake for 12–15 minutes. After cooling briefly, turn out of the pan onto a rack. If necessary, wash or wipe the mold and repeat until batter is finished. Once cooled, the madeleines can be stored in an airtight container. Serve alone or with other desserts, fruit salad, sherbet, or ice cream.

Easy Chocolate Cake
Gâteau Facile au Chocolat

Très Simple

Preparation: 15 minutes
Cooking: 25 minutes (make one
    day ahead)
Servings: 8
Equipment: double boiler,
    wooden spoon, 9-inch cake
    pan, parchment paper,
    bain-marie

INGREDIENTS

9 ounces dark semi-sweet or
    bittersweet chocolate, chopped
1 cup plus 1 tablespoon unsalted
    butter, divided use
4 eggs
1 cup plus 2 tablespoons sugar
¾ cup cake flour
1 tablespoon cocoa powder
Powdered sugar (optional)
English Cream (p. 128, optional)

Dense and rich, Easy Chocolate Cake is a chocolate lover's dream. When Monique Esquerré came to develop the recipes for la Madeleine, this was one of the best. One evening, very late, a customer came in and bought the last piece of cake. The next day he returned to order enough cakes to feed his entire staff at Neiman Marcus. During summer, try a fruit coulis with the cake.

Preheat oven to 400°. Combine chocolate with 1 cup of butter and melt slowly in a double boiler.

Remove from heat and add eggs one at a time, beating well with a wooden spoon after each addition. Continue mixing while adding sugar, then flour.

Prepare a 9-inch cake pan by cutting a round piece of parchment paper to fit the bottom. Butter the cake pan and the parchment with remaining butter. Dust with cocoa powder. Pour cake batter into the pan.

Place cake pan in a larger pan half-filled with boiling water. Bake for 25 minutes. Test center; if not cooked, bake a little longer. Center should be very moist. Remove from oven and water. Let cake sit for a day. Turn out of mold onto a serving plate. If cake will not fall out, reheat for 30 seconds over burner. Serve at room temperature. Garnish with sifted powdered sugar. May be served with English Cream.

Reci Tip—To facilitate the removal of cake from the tin after baking, place a wet cloth, folded in fourths, on the bottom of the tin. Or you can place the cake tin in cold water.

Chocolate Truffles
Truffes au Chocolat

Preparation: 25 minutes
Cooking: 10 minutes melting
time, plus 5 hours to chill
Yield: 40 truffles
Equipment: 1½-quart saucepan,
melon scoop, paper pastry
cups

INGREDIENTS

8 ounces good quality French or
Swiss chocolate, bittersweet or
semi-sweet
2 teaspoons milk
2 egg yolks
6 tablespoons unsalted butter,
softened and cut into pieces
2 teaspoons heavy cream
(optional)
⅔ cup imported or Dutch
Process powdered cocoa

This dessert truffle made from chocolate melts in your mouth. You can make these truffles for a party, package them for homemade gifts, even flavor them with a favorite liqueur. Some prefer to insert a small hazelnut into the center of each chocolate truffle. Rolling the chocolate into small balls may be difficult because the heat of your hands tends to melt the chocolate. Try using a melon scoop to form the balls. This dessert gets its name from the black truffle, a subterranean fungus shaped like a ball and the size of a walnut, which grows wild in the countryside around Périgord and Quercy. They are esteemed throughout the world as the black diamonds of gastronomy.

Melt chocolate with milk in a saucepan in a preheated 300° oven for 8–10 minutes, stirring occasionally. Remove when a smooth paste has formed. Taking care to remove the white string-like membrane from the egg yolks, add one at a time while stirring constantly. Then add butter in small lumps. Work mixture several minutes, beating by hand with a wooden spoon, until it comes to room temperature. Beat in heavy cream, if using. Allow to chill in refrigerator, covered, 5 hours or overnight.

Roll mixture into small balls the size of walnuts, then roll them in powdered cocoa. Place them in individual paper pastry cups. Arrange balls in an airtight container and keep refrigerated.

Reci Tip—To enhance the flavor in a chocolate dessert, add a tablespoon of strong hot coffee. —Lou Salmon

Chocolate Marquise Royale
Marquise Royale au Chocolat

Preparation: 25 minutes
Cooking: 8 minutes melting time,
   plus refrigeration overnight
Servings: 8
Equipment: mixer, 1½-quart
   saucepan, 4-cup loaf pan

INGREDIENTS

½ pound Swiss or French milk
   chocolate, chopped
1¼ cups unsalted butter, softened
½ cup sugar
5 very fresh eggs or substitute
   reduced cholesterol liquid
   whole eggs
English Cream (p. 128, optional)
Mint leaves and edible flowers
   for garnish

Because of the milk chocolate, the Chocolate Marquise Royale is delicate and lighter in color than most marquises. A light and fluffy texture can be achieved by using a heavy-duty electric mixer. The longer the mixture sits at room temperature, the softer it becomes—almost mousse-like. It can then be dished into individual bowls and chilled overnight. Serve with a raspberry or strawberry coulis (Fresh Fruit Sauce, p. 126).

Melt chocolate in a saucepan in preheated 300° oven. Remove from heat and cool slightly. Stir several times and add butter a little at a time. Stirring constantly, add sugar, then whole eggs, one at time. Beat 2–3 minutes between each egg. Or use a mixer with the whip attachment.

Butter a loaf pan or line with plastic wrap. Spread mixture in the pan, smoothing the top. Hit pan on counter a few times to eliminate air bubbles.

Cover and refrigerate overnight or 1 day. To unmold, dip pan rapidly into hot water. This is not necessary if using plastic wrap. Invert onto a platter. Wipe away any part that has melted. Cut into ¾-inch slices with a knife dipped in hot water and wiped dry.

This extremely fine Marquise can be served with a light English Cream. Garnish with mint leaves and edible flowers.

Reci Tip—Don't throw a vanilla bean away after use. Instead rinse, dry, and place it in the container that holds your sugar to add flavor.

Almond Lace Cookies
Tuiles aux Amandes

Preparation: 20 minutes
Cooking: 8–12 minutes
Yield: 30 cookies
Equipment: 2½-quart saucepan,
   13-inch x 18-inch baking
   sheet, parchment paper

INGREDIENTS

¾ cup unsalted butter
1 cup sugar
¼ cup light corn syrup
⅓ cup milk
2½ cups sliced almonds

Fabulous Almond Lace Cookies are crunchy, sweet, and full of almonds. Fresh Fruit Sauce (p. 126) would make a splendid addition.

Combine butter, sugar, corn syrup, and milk in a saucepan and bring to a boil. Boil for 1 minute. Remove from heat; add almonds and combine well. Let mixture cool slightly. It will become less liquid. Preheat oven to 350°.

Line a baking sheet with parchment paper. Spoon one tablespoon of mixture per cookie on the paper, flattening with the back of the spoon. Allow at least 3 inches between cookies, as they will spread. Bake for 8–12 minutes, or until the cookies are a light brown color.

Remove from oven; let cool for 2 minutes before removing from pan. Shape by placing each cookie over a custard cup to form a shell in which to place ice cream or fruit. Roll for cookie or cone shape. Fill with whipped cream and fresh fruit, and top with grated chocolate. These cookies will harden as they cool. Store in an airtight container.

—*Jean Bardet*

French Maxim—Nothing has a richer history than gastronomy, because man has been eating—everywhere he was, anytime he could get food—since the beginning of time.

Almond Tartlets with Fruit Preserves

Amandine à la Purée de Fruits

Preparation: 20 minutes
Cooking: 20–25 minutes
Servings: 4
Equipment: 5-inch tart pans,
    rolling pin, brush

Ingredients

1 recipe Sweet Tart Dough
    (p. 130)
½ cup reduced fruit purée or
    preserves (black currant,
    raspberry, apricot)
1¼ cups Almond Cream (p. 127)
3½ ounces almonds, slivered
½ cup apple or apricot jelly
Fresh fruit for garnish

You can vary this basic recipe with different fillings and a different tart dough. Vary the fruit purées or preserves depending on the season. For example, try cranberry in winter. Almond Tart Dough (p. 129) also works well. The recipe can easily be multiplied to serve more.

Roll out tart dough on a floured surface; line lightly buttered tart pans as directed on page 118. Place in refrigerator for ½ hour to chill. Preheat oven to 400°.

Cover bottom of tart dough with a layer of fruit purée or preserves. Next spread a layer of Almond Cream over the fruit. Sprinkle slivers of almonds over the cream. Bake for 20–25 minutes. When cool remove from tart pans. Melt jelly in a small pan until liquid and brush on tartlets. Garnish with fresh fruit, if desired.

Almond Tartlets

Follow recipe above but eliminate fruit purée filling. Fill each tartlet, using ½ cup Almond Cream, fill the tarts and top with additional almonds. Proceed as above with baking and glazing.

Almond Meringue Tartlets

Eliminate fruit purée from original recipe. Fill tartlets with Almond Cream as above. Beat 2 egg whites to stiff peaks, carefully incorporating ½ cup sugar to make meringue. Layer meringue on top of almond cream using a pastry bag or spoon. Bake in preheated oven at 425° for 15–20 minutes.

Raspberry Tart
Tarte aux Framboises

Preparation: 20 minutes
Cooking: 20 minutes
Servings: 6
Equipment: rolling pin, 9-inch
   tart pan, brush, 1-quart
   saucepan

INGREDIENTS

¼ recipe Almond Tart Dough
   (p. 129)
1½ pounds fresh raspberries
4 tablespoons red currant or
   raspberry jelly

Raspberry tarts, so simple to prepare and so elegant to serve, really make a statement at a party. The almond crusts showcase the berries perfectly. And for variation you can spread the tart with a layer of whipping cream before placing the berries on top. Decorate with melted white chocolate or sifted powdered sugar. Strawberries, blackberries, red currants, or black currants may be substituted for raspberries.

Roll out Almond Tart Dough on a floured surface. Line a buttered round tart pan with thinly rolled dough or pat in dough with fingertips. Prick bottom of dough to prevent air bubbles during baking.

Chill in refrigerator for 30 minutes. Bake in a preheated 400° oven for 20 minutes. Allow to cool.

Remove stems from fruit. Wash raspberries carefully in cold water. Drain and gently pat dry.

Melt fruit jelly in a saucepan, without allowing to boil. Brush a thin coating of jelly on cooled crust. Arrange raspberries, stem side down, in tart. Spread remainder of melted jelly over fruit using a brush.

Allow to stand 10 minutes before serving.

French Maxim—The art of having good taste is avoiding excess.

Apple or Pear Tart

Tarte aux Pommes ou aux Poires

Preparation: 15 minutes
Cooking: 30–40 minutes
Servings: 6
Equipment: rolling pin, 9-inch
  tart pan with removable
  bottom, parchment paper, pie
  weights or dried beans,
  1-quart saucepan

INGREDIENTS

1 recipe Sweet Tart Dough
  (p. 130)
1¼ pound tart apples or pears,
  peeled, cored, halved, and
  sliced thin
8 tablespoons unsalted butter
4 tablespoons granulated sugar
1 whole egg

You can take these classic country tarts to your next family gathering and please everyone there. They are the very essence of French country simplicity.

❧

Preheat oven to 400°. Roll pie dough out on a floured surface. Line 9-inch tart pan with dough. Place a piece of parchment paper or foil on dough and fill cavity with beans or pie weights. Pre-bake crust for 10 minutes to prevent crust from puffing. After 10 minutes remove from oven and carefully lift out the paper and weights. Fill in holes or gaps, if necessary, with raw dough. Reduce oven to 350°.

Cover bottom of tart with fruit arranged in tight decorative circles.

Melt butter over low heat, without browning it, in a saucepan. Remove from heat. Add sugar and stir until it dissolves. Beat egg with a fork and add to mixture. Pour this over the apples or pears. Bake at 350° for 30–40 minutes or until fruit is tender.

INGREDIENTS

1 recipe Sweet Tart Dough
  (p. 130)
3 tablespoons unsalted butter
1 cup sugar
3 eggs
Juice of 2 lemons and zest of
  1 lemon, about 1 tablespoon

Lemon Tart

Prepare dough and tart crust as above. Melt butter in a saucepan without browning it. Remove from heat and stir in sugar until it dissolves. Beat eggs with a fork in a bowl. Add lemon juice, zest, and sugar/butter mixture, beating with a wooden spoon. Pour into pre-baked crust and bake in preheated 350° oven for 20–25 minutes.

Quick Apple Tart
Tarte Fine Minute aux Pommes

Très Simple

Preparation: 30 minutes, plus
   1 hour refrigeration
Cooking: 20 minutes
Servings: 8
Equipment: bowl, rolling pin,
   13-inch x 18-inch baking sheet

INGREDIENTS

2 cups flour
10 tablespoons softened unsalted
   butter
Pinch of salt
¼ cup water
4 Golden Delicious apples,
   peeled, cored, halved, and
   sliced thin
1½ cups plus 2 tablespoons
   sugar, divided use
6 tablespoons unsalted butter,
   cut in pieces, chilled
English Cream (p. 128, optional)

The Marquise Sue de Brantes, who gave me this recipe at the Château du Fresne, is one of my dearest friends. During my life, it always seemed that when I faced a door of opportunity, Sue was always there to open it for me. It was she, in fact, who was directly responsible for my coming to the United States and establishing la Madeleine.　　　　*—Patrick Esquerré*

Prepare pastry by mixing flour, softened butter, pinch of salt, and water. Mix until just combined, no longer. Dough should be a smooth paste. Flatten dough slightly, wrap in wax paper, and chill in refrigerator for 1 hour. Preheat oven to 475°.

Divide dough in 2 equal pieces. Roll each piece to 7½ inches in diameter and ⅛ inch thick. Place each on a buttered baking sheet. Pinch up the sides of the dough ever so slightly to keep liquids in while baking.

Arrange apple slices on the dough circles, overlapping them in a regular pattern. Sprinkle each tart with ¾ cup of sugar and 3 tablespoons of butter, cut into pieces.

Bake tarts for approximately 20 minutes or until top is caramelized. After about 15 minutes, sprinkle each tart with 1 tablespoon of sugar. Return to finish baking. Serve as is or with English Cream.　　　*—Marquise Sue de Brantes, Château du Fresne*

French Maxim—Charm is the reward we receive for being kind, cheerful, always amiable, always in a good mood.
　　　　　　　　　　　—Hélène Treskine

Madame Henriette's Tart
Tarte Madame Henriette

Preparation: 40 minutes
Cooking: 55 minutes
Servings: 6
Equipment: 1½-quart saucepan,
    9-inch tart pan

INGREDIENTS

½ recipe (10 ounces) Puff Pastry
    Dough (pp. 131–32)
1 pound apples, peeled, cored,
    and chopped
¾ pound apples, peeled, cored,
    and sliced thin
5 tablespoons sugar, divided use
4 tablespoons apple or currant
    jelly

Madame Henriette, my boyhood nanny, is one of the finest cooks I have ever known. When she made her wonderful apple tarts, it was always a very special event. Our friends would do everything they could to get themselves invited to dinner. Even though the recipe is a very simple one, no one seems to make tarts as delicious as Madame Henriette's.

Roll out dough on lightly floured surface. Line tart pan with the dough. Trim edges if necessary. Poke holes in dough with a fork to prevent puffing. Chill in refrigerator. Preheat oven to 400°.

Cook chopped apples in saucepan slowly, covered, over low heat until reduced to a thick purée, about 25 minutes. Set aside to cool.

Remove dough from refrigerator and sprinkle with 2 tablespoons of sugar. Spread apple purée evenly over the sugared dough. Arrange apple slices in a concentric, overlapping pattern, starting at the outer edge and finishing in the center. Sprinkle with 3 tablespoons of sugar. Bake for 30 minutes. Before serving, melt the jelly and brush on the top for a glaze.

Aunt Lucie's Tart

Prepare crust and apple purée as above, adding 3 tablespoons of sugar to the chopped apples. Peel 2 oranges and cut into thin slices. Omit cut apples and top apple purée with the overlapping orange slices. Bake tart in a preheated 350° oven for 30 minutes. Beat 3 egg whites in a mixer until stiff, adding ½ cup sugar gradually toward the end. Remove tart from oven and spread or pipe meringue on top, covering oranges entirely. Return to oven and bake 15 minutes, until meringue is golden.

Emperor's Omelette
Kaiserschmarren

Très Simple

Preparation: 15 minutes
Cooking: 15–30 minutes
Servings: 6–8
Equipment: 6-quart bowl, mixer,
    12- to 14-inch omelette pan,
    stainless steel kettle, 6-quart
    saucepan

INGREDIENTS

2 cups milk
7 tablespoons flour, sifted
8 eggs, separated
1 tablespoon or more of sugar
1 pinch of salt
7 tablespoons unsalted butter,
    melted
¼ cup raisins
1 tablespoon rum
2 tablespoons unsalted butter,
    divided use
½ cup powdered sugar

INGREDIENTS

4 pounds ripe dark plums
4 cups sugar
¼ teaspoon cinnamon
1 whole clove

Yield: 5 pints

The Alsace region of France has been ruled at times by Germany and Austria, leaving a culinary influence unseen anywhere else in France. Austrian Emperor Franz-Josef had unusual taste when it came to food. This omelette, sweetened with raisins, powdered sugar, and rum, and served with a compote of plums, was one of his favorites. In fact, he insisted it be served for dinner 365 days a year.

In a large mixing bowl whisk flour into milk. When smooth, mix in egg yolks, sugar, salt, melted butter, raisins, and rum, blending well. Using a mixer, beat egg whites until stiff. Stir ¼ of the egg whites into the yolk mixture, then gently fold in the remaining whites.

Heat 1 tablespoon of unsalted butter in an omelette pan or a skillet. Pour in the batter to a depth of ¼ inch. Cook until the underside has a crust. Flip omelette over and cook until set. If omelette is too large to turn over, run it under a preheated broiler to cook the top. Turn omelette out onto a serving platter. Repeat process, if necessary, to finish batter. Tear cooked omelette into pieces onto a serving plate. Sprinkle lavishly with powdered sugar and serve with the Compote of Plums.

—*Stanley Marcus*

Compote of Plums

Wash and pit plums. Put them in a heavy stainless steel kettle. Cover them with sugar; add the cinnamon and clove; cover with a cloth and let stand overnight. The next day cook the plums over low heat for approximately 2 hours, stirring occasionally to keep them from burning. Cook until the fruit becomes translucent and the syrup is heavy. Remove the clove. Serve with the omelette or seal and store for later use.

—*Stanley Marcus*

Lemon Soufflé
Soufflé au Citron

Preparation: 20 minutes
Cooking: 12 minutes
Servings: 4
Equipment: 2-quart bowl, whisk,
   mixer, 9-inch square baking
   dish, pastry bag

INGREDIENTS

4 large lemons
4 eggs, separated
4 tablespoons sugar
1 tablespoon lemon juice
Juice of 1 orange
1 teaspoon Grand Marnier
   (optional)
1 teaspoon lemon zest (optional)
Powdered sugar for decoration

Lemon Soufflé is a perfect ending to any summertime meal. Prepare the lemons and egg yolk mixture ahead of time, completing the rest as you near serving time. You can use a grapefruit spoon to help clean out the lemons. If there is extra soufflé mixture, cook it in a buttered, sugared ramekin. Garnish with lemon leaves and an edible flower.

Slice off the top of each lemon, or cut lemons in half, allowing 2 halves per person. Remove pulp from lemons and reserve for another use. The empty lemons will serve as soufflé molds. Cut a small slice off bottoms so they will stand nicely. Place in a baking dish. Preheat oven to 375°.

In a bowl mix together the egg yolks and sugar, using a wooden spoon, until creamy. Add lemon juice, orange juice, and Grand Marnier, if using. Add lemon zest, if using. In a mixer beat egg whites to stiff peaks, and fold gently into yolk mixture. Fill each lemon with mixture. Bake for 12 minutes. Sprinkle with sifted powdered sugar and serve immediately.

Reci Tip—To get more juice out of a lemon, put it in boiling water for 5 minutes.

Pear Soufflé
Soufflé aux Poires

Preparation: 20 minutes
Cooking: 20 minutes
Servings: 4
Equipment: saucepan, blender, whisk, bowl, 1-quart soufflé dish, bain-marie

INGREDIENTS

4 pears, peeled, seeded, and quartered
1 egg yolk
1½ cups sugar
1 tablespoon Poire William
4 egg whites, beaten stiff

This is a very aromatic and flavorful soufflé for when pears are in season. Poire William is a Pear eau-de-vie available in liquor stores. The soufflé may also be made in individual molds.

Preheat oven to 425°. Cook pears for 5 minutes in a saucepan over medium heat until softened, then purée in a blender. Transfer purée to a bowl and add egg yolk, sugar, and Poire William, blending well.

Fold pear mixture into stiffly beaten egg whites. Butter and sugar a 1-quart soufflé mold; pour in soufflé. Place in a bain-marie. Bake for 15–20 minutes.

Reci Tip—Pears and tomatoes will keep longer if you store them with the stems up. Apples keep longer with stems down.

Pears Poached in Red Wine
Poires Pochées au Vin Rouge

Très Simple

Preparation: 15 minutes the first
　　day, 10 minutes the following
　　day
Cooking: 25 minutes the first
　　day, 10–15 minutes the next
Servings: 8
Equipment: saucepan tall
　　enough to hold pears upright

INGREDIENTS

8 Bosc or Anjou pears, of a uni-
　　form size and ripeness
1 bottle good red wine
1 cup black or red currant jelly
1¼ cups Crème de Cassis liqueur
1 cinnamon stick
½ cup sugar or to taste
Ground cinnamon to taste
5 ounces almond slivers, lightly
　　toasted

If you are getting ready for a party, you can prepare Pears Poached in Red Wine in advance. The rich sauce is intense and flavorful, very appealing to the eyes, and a delight to the palate. Serve with English Cream (p. 128) for a contrast of colors. Garnish with mint or orange leaves and an edible flower.

The first day, peel pears, but leave stem attached. Stand them up in a saucepan just large enough to hold them close together. To the pan add wine, black currant jelly, Crème de Cassis, cinnamon stick, and about ½ cup of sugar and bring to boil. Skim off any froth, reduce heat and simmer, covered, for 25 minutes or until tender. Check pears with a very thin skewer to see if tender. Allow pears to cool in liquid. Refrigerate in the cooking liquid overnight.

The next day, remove pears from liquid. Taste and add more sugar, if desired. Pour liquid into a saucepan and reduce by half over medium heat. Set aside and allow to cool. Remove cinnamon stick.

Arrange pears in individual bowls or in a large bowl. Pour some of the cooking liquid over each portion. Garnish with a sprinkle of cinnamon and lightly toasted almond slivers.

Reci Tip—Easy whipped cream: put a cocktail shaker in the freezer for 15 minutes. Pour chilled heavy cream into shaker with a teaspoon of cold water. Shake vigorously until no sound is heard.

Fruit Sherbet
Sorbet aux Fruits

Très Simple

Preparation: 10 minutes plus
    freezing time
Cooking: 15 minutes
Servings: 6
Equipment: ice cream freezer,
    2½-quart saucepan

INGREDIENTS

1½ cups sugar
2¼ cups water
2 pounds fresh fruit (cherries,
    strawberries, raspberries, red
    currants, black currants,
    blueberries, blackberries,
    mangoes)
Juice of 1 lemon
Fresh Fruit Sauce (optional)

Fruit Sherbet is the delicate way that French gourmets enjoy summer fruits when they are caught up in the warm sunshine of summertime. For a beautiful presentation, you can serve several colors of sherbert on a contrasting fresh fruit coulis. Garnish with mint leaves or edible flowers.

Combine sugar and water in a saucepan over medium heat to make a syrup. Boil until syrup begins to adhere to a wooden spoon in droplets, about 15 minutes. Allow to cool. This step may be prepared a day ahead of time.

Wash fruit; remove and discard stems and any seeds or stones. Purée in a blender. Add lemon juice.

In a bowl mix syrup and fruit purée together in equal parts. Pour into an ice cream freezer and freeze according to freezer directions.

As an alternative, just before sherbet begins to harden, while ice cream freezer is running, add a jelly complementary to the fruit being used.

This sherbet should be kept in freezer. Serve with Fresh Fruit Sauce (p. 126).

Reci Tip—A decoration tip: If you are serving a dish that needs to be very, very cold, place some little edible flowers on the plate, spray them with water, and put the plate in the freezer for 1 or 2 hours. When the dish is served, the plate looks like it is ringed with crystal flowers. —Monique Binet

Fresh Fruit Sauce
Coulis de Fruits Frais

Très Simple

Preparation: 15 minutes
Cooking: not required
Yield: 2½ cups
Equipment: blender

INGREDIENTS

1 pound fresh fruit, washed,
  stemmed, peeled, and stoned
  (strawberries, raspberries,
  blackberries, mangoes,
  peaches, etc.)
1–1½ cups sugar
Juice of 1 lemon (optional)

Fresh Fruit Sauce—a coulis that is delicate and delicious—is used at la Madeleine French Bakery & Café. Bursting with the flavors of fresh fruit, the sauce will enhance, decorate, or add to any dish that it accompanies. If the fruit is naturally sweet, simply cut back on the sugar, beginning with one-half cup. Keep tasting and adding sugar as necessary.

Place fruit or fruit pulp in a blender and purée together with sugar for at least 10 minutes to produce a smooth and delicious fruit sauce. Use lemon juice with fruits that have a tendency to turn brown.

The sauce can be kept at least 8 days in an airtight container in the refrigerator or longer in the freezer.

Serve with cakes, sherbets, ice cream, and fresh fruit.
—*Rémy Schaal, Head Chef, la Madeleine*

Reci Tip—To preserve the color, texture, and taste of frozen fruit, roll 1 pound of fresh fruit in 1/4 cup of sugar prior to freezing. Freeze fruit in a single layer. When frozen, transfer to a more compact container and seal.

Oysters in a Bowl (p. 83)

Top: Salmon in Parchment (p. 85); bottom: Scallops on a Skewer (p. 87) and French Pasta (p. 105)

Filet of Sole and Salmon Braised in Cream (p. 86)

Almond Lace Cookies (p. 115) with Raspberry Sauce (p. 109)

Chocolate Marquise Royale (p. 114)
with English Cream (p. 128) and
Raspberry Sauce (p. 109)

A whole Raspberry Tart (p. 117) and a slice of
Quick Apple Tart (p. 119)

Pears Poached in Red Wine (p. 124)

Top left: Madeleine Cakes (p. 111); bottom left: Lemon Soufflé (p. 122); above: Hazelnut Cake (p. 109)

Easy Chocolate Cake (p. 112)

Almond Cream
Crème d'Amandes

Très Simple

Preparation: 5 minutes
Cooking: as required
Yield: about 2½ cups
Equipment: mixer or whisk,
   mixer with 3-quart bowl,
   blender or food processor

INGREDIENTS

¾ cup granulated sugar, divided
   use
10 tablespoons unsalted butter,
   softened
2 eggs, room temperature
1 cup blanched almonds
3½ tablespoons flour
3 tablespoons rum
¼ teaspoon vanilla extract

This delicious filling is used for the Almond Tartlets (p. 116). It may also be used in other tarts, cooked for about 20 minutes, and topped with fresh fruit.

Beat 10 tablespoons sugar and unsalted butter together in a mixer at medium speed until a frothy cream is obtained. Add eggs, one at a time, beating well after each addition.

Place almonds in container of blender or food processor with 2 tablespoons of sugar and pulverize to a powder.

Mix powdered almond and flour and add to the eggs and sugar. Then add rum and vanilla. Beat until well combined. This cream may be used right away or covered and chilled for use within 2 days. Return to room temperature before using.

Reci Tip—To prevent a fresh fruit salad from wilting in summertime, use a cold watermelon as a bowl.
—Albertine Decaux

English Cream
Crème Anglaise

Preparation: 5 minutes
Cooking: 30 minutes
Yield: 1 quart
Equipment: 2½-quart saucepan,
  whisk, strainer, bowl, double
  boiler

INGREDIENTS

3¼ cups milk
1 packet vanilla sugar or
  1 teaspoon vanilla extract
6 egg yolks
1¼ cups sugar

English Cream is recognized as a classic, all-purpose dessert sauce and can be prepared a day ahead. It can be flavored as desired, using coffee, a liqueur, or even nuts. Serve it with anything chocolate, as well as with fruit desserts, cakes, or tarts. You will be able to find vanilla sugar in French or German specialty stores.

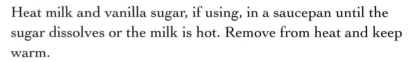

Heat milk and vanilla sugar, if using, in a saucepan until the sugar dissolves or the milk is hot. Remove from heat and keep warm.

Heat water in the bottom of a double boiler to simmering. Whisk egg yolks with sugar in the top of the double boiler, off heat. As mixture turns pale yellow, add hot milk, a little at a time, whisking rapidly so that egg yolks do not cook. Place top of double boiler over simmering water, stirring mixture with a wooden spoon until the moment the wooden spoon becomes coated. Sauce will become noticeably thicker. Do not boil or sauce will separate.

Remove from heat. Pour cream into a cold bowl and continue to stir for a few moments to assist cooling. Stir in vanilla extract now, if using. Cool in refrigerator before serving.

Reci Tip—should English Cream begin to boil and separate, quickly pour into a metal shaker or a 1/2-gallon glass bottle. Taking care not to be burned, shake mixture vigorously. Strain through a sieve. The cream will be saved.

Almond Tart Dough
Pâte Sablée aux Amandes

Preparation: 15 minutes
Cooking: as required
Yield: approximately four 9-inch
   tart shells
Equipment: 3-quart mixing
   bowl, blender or food
   processor, pastry blender
   (optional)

INGREDIENTS

1½ cups blanched almonds
4½ cups flour
Zest of 1 lemon
¾ cup sugar, divided use
1 pinch salt
2 cups unsalted butter, cut into
   large cubes and refrigerated
   until ready for use
1 whole egg
2 egg yolks
3 tablespoons rum

You may find that it is difficult to roll out the Almond Tart Dough and get it into the pie pan without tearing. But tears are really no problem. Just go ahead and pat the dough in the pan, patching up any holes that might have appeared. It is a soft, pliable dough that makes an excellent crust. A food processor expedites the mixing; just be sure you don't overmix.

Place almonds in container of blender or food processor with 2 tablespoons of sugar and pulverize to a powder.

In a mixing bowl mix together flour, almonds, sugar, lemon zest, remaining sugar, and salt. Push mixture to sides of bowl, creating a well in the center. Place butter, the whole egg, 2 egg yolks, and rum in the well. Work mixture with a fork, pastry blender, or floured hands until all ingredients have been thoroughly incorporated. Form dough into ball before dividing it. Unused dough may be kept in refrigerator or frozen for future use. To keep dough, flatten pieces between sheets of wax paper, then wrap in plastic.

This dough may be used for raspberry, strawberry, red or black currant, blueberry tarts, and almond tartlets.   —*Jean Lenoir*

Reci Tip—French coffee has always been a great ingredient in our life, stimulating our energy and our imagination. We like Italian espresso very much, but it is a very condensed Arabica served in doll-sized cups. You need to drink two cups. American coffee is good to sponge your thirst, but it has a tendency to flood the stomach. French coffee is a good compromise.

Sweet Tart Dough
Pâte à Tarte Sucrée

Preparation: 10 minutes, plus 1½
    hours to chill
Cooking: as required
Servings: 1 9-inch tart crust
Equipment: 2-quart bowl, fork
    and spoon, rolling pin

INGREDIENTS

½ cup plus 2 tablespoons sugar
1¼ cups flour
1 egg
½ cup unsalted butter, cut into
    small pieces, chilled

Sweet tarts have long been popular throughout France. This dough makes a wonderful crust. Make extra and freeze between sheets of wax paper. Each family in France, it seems, has its own special filling to add to a tart, so we recommend that you use this dough and create a tart that can become famous in your own home.

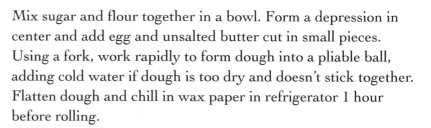

Mix sugar and flour together in a bowl. Form a depression in center and add egg and unsalted butter cut in small pieces. Using a fork, work rapidly to form dough into a pliable ball, adding cold water if dough is too dry and doesn't stick together. Flatten dough and chill in wax paper in refrigerator 1 hour before rolling.

Roll out dough on a floured surface with a rolling pin. Line pie pan with dough. Roll dough loosely over the rolling pin, then place over the pan and unroll gently to transfer it from the surface to the pan; carefully press to fit sides of pan. Set aside for ½ hour in refrigerator to chill.

Up to ½ cup additional flour may be added if dough is too wet. This is a very fragile dough, so if dough is too sticky to roll out, pat it into tart pans with fingers dipped in flour.

Reci Tip—Hiccup Remedy: swallow a mixture of 1 teaspoon of sugar with a few drops of vinegar.

Puff Pastry Dough
Pâte Feuilletée

Preparation: 2 hours
Cooking: as required
Yield: 23 ounces
Equipment: rolling pin, 2-quart
   mixing bowl

INGREDIENTS

2 cups flour
¾ cup ice water
1 teaspoon salt
1¼ cups unsalted butter, chilled

When making Puff Pastry Dough, find a surface in the kitchen that is cool, because the key to this technique is keeping the dough cold. A marble slab is perfect for rolling out dough. Try the recipe at least once; it is well worth the effort. If, however, you do not have the time to make the recipe at home, there is puff pastry dough available in the frozen foods section of grocery stores.

Dough should always be prepared in a cool room. Place flour in mixing bowl, pushing flour to sides to form a well in the center. Pour water and salt into well. Work dough gently, either with a spatula or fingers, until it forms a soft dough. Do not overwork. Roll out dough on a floured board to obtain a rectangle about 14 inches x 10 inches x ³⁄₁₆ inch.

Cut butter into small pieces, or cut sticks lengthwise into slices and place on dough side by side, covering the left two-thirds of dough. Fold dough over into thirds, the right side in, then the left, to cover butter completely, still maintaining a rectangular shape. Wrap in wax paper or foil to prevent drying out. Chill in refrigerator for 10 minutes, then roll again: place unwrapped dough on surface with long open side facing away from you, folded side toward you. Roll dough to a 10-inch x 14-inch rectangle or larger, taking care not to allow butter to ooze out or puncture the dough. (Rolling stretches the gluten.) Fold dough in thirds again, right side then left. Wrap and chill in refrigerator for 15 minutes to relax the gluten.

Now follow a sequence which will be repeated for a total of 5 times. For each successive rolling, the dough will be placed on the surface with the long open side away from you, thereby turning it 90° each time. This stretches the gluten in both directions. Roll dough out, as before, on a lightly floured, cool surface to a rectangle about 10 inches x 14 inches x ½ inch, maintaining square corners. Roll smoothly and evenly to keep butter from getting too warm. (Keep track of how many times you roll out the dough.) Rewrap and chill dough each time, always about 15 minutes. The more the dough is rolled and folded, the flakier the crust will be. After the final rest, dough is ready for use.

QUICK
RECIPES

Salads
Marinated Yellow and Red Peppers
Rotisserie Chicken Salad
Composed Salad
Salad with Bacon

First Course
Radish Canapés

Entrées
Chicken Dijon
Patrick's Duck Breast
Steaks with Roquefort
Lamb Chops with Basil Butter
Salmon Croque Monsieur
Party Pork Tenderloins
Tuna Steaks with Onion Purée

Vegetables
Quick Endives
Stuffed Potatoes
Jean-Luc's Pot-au-Feu de Légumes
Creamed Pasta with Basil

Desserts
Melon Surprise
Fruit Tabbouleh
Coupe Martinique
Plum Express
Petits Fours Glacés
Strawberry Preserves

Très . . . Très . . . Très . . . Simple Recipes

Too often we are in a hurry, especially when it is time to prepare a good meal. For that reason we have included this sampling of easy and tasty recipes. Even if you are a novice cook you will have no trouble at all preparing them for family, for guests, or for yourself when you want a creative alternative to a sandwich.

Salads

Marinated Yellow and Red Peppers

Cut 6 peppers (3 of each color) in half, core, and discard seeds. Place peppers under the broiler or on an outdoor grill until skin blisters and puffs. Let peppers cool, peel and cut into strips. Place in a shallow dish and cover with 1 cup of extra virgin olive oil mixed with juice of 1 lemon. Salt and pepper to taste. Sprinkle with minced fresh herbs of choice. Serve as a salad, with or without lettuce, on pieces of toasted French bread that have been rubbed with garlic, or as a topping for grilled chicken. Serves 6.

Rotisserie Chicken Salad

Stephanie Garb of Houston sent this easy recipe utilizing the flavorful, spicy chicken served at la Madeleine. To 3 cups cooked diced chicken, add 1 cup each of chopped celery and apple, along with 2 green onions sliced. Moisten with ½ cup mayonnaise. The spices on the rotisserie chicken are the perfect complement for the apples. Serve with toasted baguette rounds or as a salad, with croutons. Serves 4.

Composed Salad

Prepare 1 cup of Sherry Vinaigrette (p. 52) and set aside. Line a salad bowl or 6 individual plates with curly leaf lettuce. Arrange artfully on top the following ingredients: 1 celery heart (with leaves) cut lengthwise into pieces, a diced red apple (rubbed with lemon), 6 artichoke hearts, 2 sliced bananas, 12 sliced radishes and 18 walnuts. Season salad with Vinaigrette, salt, and pepper to taste. Garnish with fresh herbs and edible flowers. Serves 6.

Salad with Bacon

Prepare 1 cup of Pungent Vinaigrette (p. 51), adding to it 1 minced shallot and 1 minced garlic clove. Sauté 16 small cubes of day-old bread in a pan with 3 tablespoons of unsalted butter to make croutons and set aside. To the pan add 4 slices of thick bacon cut into strips and sauté. To 1 head of curly lettuce such as frisée, escarole, endive, or Boston add ¾ cup of Vinaigrette and toss. Scatter over the salad the hot croutons, cooked bacon, 3 diced hard-boiled eggs, chopped parsley, and remaining Vinaigrette. Makes 4 servings.

First Course

Radish Canapés

Don't throw out the fresh, pretty green tops of radishes. Instead chop the greens finely and mix with softened unsalted butter. Remove crusts from French bread and cut bread into small pieces. Spread bread with radish butter and top with a decorative radish slice.

Entrées

Chicken Dijon

In a large sauté pan brown 2 chickens cut into serving pieces in 2 tablespoons unsalted butter. When browned add 2 unpeeled cloves of garlic, cover, and simmer for 20 minutes. Skim the fat from pan juices. In a bowl whisk together 4 tablespoons Dijon mustard, 4 tablespoons tomato paste, and 5 tablespoons white wine. Add to the chicken, stirring well. Cook chicken another 25 minutes. In a small saucepan reduce 8 tablespoons of wine vinegar to 2. Add to chicken along with 2 tablespoons Worchestershire Sauce. The sauce may be served as is or enriched with ½ cup cream. Remove garlic before serving to 6 guests.

Patrick's Duck Breast

Heat a pan just large enough for duck over medium heat. Place duck breast skin side down. Cook slowly to render fat for 10 minutes, removing fat as it accumulates. Season with salt and freshly ground pepper to taste. Turn and cook 3–5 minutes on the other side. Garnish with parsley. Cut-up vegetables may be added to the pan as the duck cooks. Each duck breast serves 1.

Steaks with Roquefort

Cream 1 cup unsalted butter with 2⅔ cups of Roquefort cheese and 1 teaspoon of arrowroot; place in a double boiler and heat gently until you obtain a smooth, thick cream. Pan sauté or charcoal grill 6 thick steaks, (which have been seasoned with salt and freshly ground pepper to taste) for 7–10 minutes, or until cooked. Serve steaks with cheese sauce. Serves 6.

Lamb Chops with Basil Butter

Combine in a mortar or food processor 1 clove garlic, 8 fresh basil leaves, 3 sprigs parsley, and 6 tablespoons softened unsalted butter. Crush and combine well. Set aside (or freeze for future use). Season 4 thick lamb chops with extra virgin olive oil, rosemary, savory, thyme, salt, and freshly ground pepper, to taste. Set aside ½ hour. Broil under preheated broiler or on charcoal grill until done, then top the chops with basil butter at serving time. Serve with grilled-in-the-oven tomatoes topped with the same herbs and some extra virgin olive oil. Serves 4.

Salmon Croque Monsieur

Using square sourdough bread, spread two slices lightly with crème fraîche, mayonnaise, or sour cream. Lay slices of smoked salmon or cooked salmon on cream. Top with the other slice of bread, crème fraîche to the inside. Top sandwich with grated Gruyère cheese and broil for 3 minutes until cheese is melted and golden. Serves 1.

Party Pork Tenderloins

Simply brush tenderloins liberally with apricot or peach preserves and brown evenly in a lightly oiled ovenproof skillet. Finish off pork in a preheated 350° oven for 20–25 minutes. Slice in medallions. Serve hot or cold. Serves 2 per tenderloin.

Tuna Steaks with Onion Purée

Using a casserole, heat ¼ cup extra virgin olive oil and gently brown 3 chopped onions, 1 minced garlic clove, and 2 chopped shallots. Remove from heat and place 4 fresh tuna steaks on top of the onion mixture in a single layer. Season with salt and freshly ground pepper, to taste. Mix 2 cups of good quality spaghetti sauce or the Fresh Tomato Sauce (p. 91) with 2 table-spoons of cream and ¼ cup of Scotch whisky. Pour this mixture over the fish and bake 30 minutes in a preheated 325° oven, or until fish is cooked. Serves 4.

Vegetables

Quick Endives

Clean 2 pounds Belgian endives, drain, dry, and slice into ½-inch circles. Melt 6 tablespoons unsalted butter in a skillet, adding endives and 1 tablespoon sugar. Cook, stirring often, until sugar begins to caramelize and endives are tender and golden, about 20 minutes. Serve with meats or omelettes. Serves up to 6.

Stuffed Potatoes

Bake or boil 8 baking potatoes until tender, taking care not to split the skin. Cut a circular hole in the top of each potato and scoop out contents. Set skins aside. Mash potato quickly with 2⅔ cups crumbled Roquefort cheese, ¾ cup unsalted butter, 6 scallions (include green tops), several sprigs of minced parsley, salt, freshly ground pepper to taste, and 2½ teaspoons of paprika. Refill potato skins with mixture and bake in a pre-heated 400° oven about 20 minutes or until hot. Serves 8.

Jean-Luc's Pot-au-Feu de Légumes

Combine 4 quarts water, 2 quartered white onions, 1 teaspoon thyme, 3 whole cloves, 1 chopped leek, 1 bay leaf, 3 parsley sprigs, 1 teaspoon salt, and freshly ground pepper. Boil together for 15 minutes. Strain bouillon and discard (or eat) the vegetables. In the bouillon, poach ½ pound each of the following vegetables separately until tender and set aside (may be prepared a day ahead): small new potatoes, carrot sticks, quartered turnips, broccoli florets, cubed zucchini, and green peas. At serving time reheat bouillon with all the vegetables. Serve in deep bowls to 4 guests. Some chopped, fresh herbs make a great garnish.

Creamed Pasta with Basil

Bring 2½ quarts salted water, to which 1 tablespoon extra virgin olive oil has been added, to a boil. Add 8 ounces fettuccine and boil until just cooked, about 10 minutes. Meanwhile mince together 1 large clove of garlic with 20 large fresh basil leaves. Pour pasta into a colander and rinse with cold water. In the still-warm saucepan heat 4 tablespoons heavy cream and 2 tablespoons unsalted butter, then add the basil mixture, salt, freshly ground pepper to taste, and the noodles. Reheat and serve immediately with 1⅓ cups grated Gruyère cheese. Serves 4 as side dish or 2 as entrée.

Desserts

Melon Surprise

Using a hollowed-out honeydew melon or watermelon as a container, fill with mixed fresh fruit flavored with mint, white wine, and Grand Marnier. Replace top of melon; set aside 2 hours. To serve, place filled melon on a bed of crushed ice. Freeze some fresh flowers in ice cubes and place on crushed ice as decoration, along with mint or lemon leaves.

Fruit Tabbouleh

Bring to a boil 1 cup water, ½ cup white wine, ½ cup sugar, 2 tea bags, and 5 mint leaves. Pour mixture over 1½ cups semolina couscous, mix, allow the grains to swell and absorb the liquid, then fluff with a fork. Remove tea bags and set aside while preparing the rest of the ingredients. Dice ¾-pound assorted seasonal fruit and mix gently together into the couscous. Serve to 5 people in individual bowls, garnished with fresh mint leaves and English Cream (p. 128).

Coupe Martinique

This delicious adult sundae is made by placing 2 or 3 scoops of vanilla ice cream in large individual glass goblets. Top with pieces or slices of fresh pineapple, slices of banana, and drizzles of Grand Marnier; whip heavy cream with sugar and top the sundae with whipped cream and cherries. Makes 1 sundae.

Plum Express

Place plums that have been cut in half and pitted on a broiler pan, skin side up. Cover with sugar and broil until sugar caramelizes and plums have softened. Serve as is or with Raspberry Sauce (p. 109) and snipped fresh mint for dessert.

Petits Fours Glacés

Form 1 pound of almond paste (marzipan, available in the grocery store), into small balls about ½ inch in diameter. Select fruit to use, such as dried prunes, dried dates, cherries in syrup, or pecans. Replace the pits of the fruits with the balls of almond paste (removing excess if needed). Re-form fruit to its original shape or place balls of almond paste between pecan halves and press to hold. Set aside in the refrigerator overnight. The next day prepare caramel by combining ¾ cup sugar, 4 tablespoons water, and 1 teaspoon vinegar in a 1-quart saucepan. Bring to a boil and simmer until syrup turns a light tea color. Have ready an oiled, very smooth surface and several wooden skewers. When it becomes the correct color, remove syrup from heat and set pan on an incline. Using wooden skewers, dip prepared fruit and nuts into syrup rapidly and transfer to oiled surface. Makes about 50 large or 100 small petits fours.

Strawberry Preserves

Wash, stem, and hull 3 pounds of fresh strawberries. Cut in half, if necessary. Set aside. Combine 4½ cups of sugar with the juice of 1 lemon and boil until sugar dissolves and mixture becomes a syrup, about 6 minutes after a boil is reached. Pour strawberries into the syrup, stir well, and boil for 10 minutes. Watch carefully to make sure the fruit does not boil over. When cooked, skim off any foam, pour mixture into sterilized jars, and seal. Unsealed jars may be refrigerated for up to 3 months.

A GUIDE TO FRENCH WINES

The Legacy of French Wines

There is no monogamy as far as wine and food are concerned. Each dish can have several wines that will go well with it. This guide will help ensure there is total harmony between a meal and the wine.

There are wonderful American wines, as well as great wines from other countries, that would be just as suitable as French wines. We are only emphasizing French wines with French country cooking because French wines are what we know best.

Too often red wine is served too warm and white wine too cold. The term "room temperature" comes from France, where wine was historically brought from the cellars of castles to be served that particular night, and generally the rooms were colder.

"Room temperature" for red wine thus is 65°. And white wine should be at the temperature of the cellar, 50–55°.

Which Wine, Which Food

SOUP
It is recommended that a very, very light country wine, a Provence wine, for instance, be served with soup.

SALAD
If you have wine vinegar in the dressing, it is practically impossible to have wine with salad, because vinegar fights with the taste of the wine. As a result, the best beverage to drink is Château-la-Pompe (which in French means water).

If there is no wine vinegar in the dressing, you can serve a very light red, white, or rosé wine. Recommended are a light Sauvignon from Loire, very light Entre-Deux-Mers from Bordeaux, a lesser appellation Bordeaux, light red Beaujolais, or a nice, light Côtes-du-Rhône. All should be served a little cooler than usual, around 60° for red and 50° for white. A white Alsace would be a nice match, like a Sylvaner or Pinot Blanc.

SHELLFISH
If the shellfish is not prepared with a sauce, serve a very dry white wine, such as a Muscadet, Sancerre, dry Vouvray, or white Beaujolais. If sauce is used, however, you will want a richer wine, such as white Graves, white Burgundy, or white Alsace (Sylvaner, Reisling, or Pinot Gris).

FISH
As a rule always serve white wine with fish. If, however, there is red wine in the sauce, then you should serve the same red wine.

If the fish is grilled, you need a simpler wine, such as a small Graves, simple Chardonnay, white Côtes-du-Rhône, or white Provence.

Fish prepared with a sauce calls for a heavier wine. Use more complex wines, like a Meursault or Chablis premier cru, with more complex sauces.

There is no absolute rule. It is all a matter of taste, and you should experiment with the basic rules.

MEAT
As a rule red wine should be served with red meat without exception.

White meat generally needs white wine, especially a deep, powerful wine such as white Hermitage or white Alsace. However, white meat can be served with a red wine as long as it is light red wine, served slightly cooler than usual (around 60°).

Beef • Serve any kind of red wine. They are all good with beef. If the beef is grilled, use a simple wine. With a complex beef dish you need a heavier wine.

Veal • Serve a lighter, more delicate, red wine, such as a St.-Julien, a Margaux, or a nice Côtes-Rôtie or Burgundy.

Chicken • Serve with any light wine, red or white, such as Beaujolais, Côtes-du-Rhône, dry Vouvray, or Pouilly Fumé.

Lamb • Serve with a Bordeaux, such as St.-Emilion, Pomerol, Hermitage, Côtes-du-Rhône, or Châteauneuf-du-Pape.

Pork • Pork goes well with any type of wine, white or red. Pork's relatively neutral flavor allows wine to take on its full flavor without competing with the flavor of the meat.

Game • Serve a very strong, heavier, sophisticated red wine, particularly the greatest Bordeaux, Burgundy, or Rhône that you have. It can create fireworks in your mouth.

VEGETABLES
Serve a simple wine, a fresh light white or red.

CHEESE
Goat cheese goes better with white wine, but in general cheese can be served with either white or red wine. Ideally, you need to drink the wine that comes from the same region as the cheese.

DESSERT
Serve with a sweet wine, such as the late harvest Alsace, Bordeaux, Touraine, Muscat de Beaunes-de-Venise, sweet Vouvray, or Champagne demi-sec (which is in fact, quite sweet).

Easy-to-Find French Wines

The following is a guide to help you select a good wine from a distinct region in France. These wines are good values and can be found in any store that features good French wines.

ALSACIAN WINES (white)

• Sylvaner and Pinot Blanc
Fresh, relatively acidic, and with a discreet fruit taste. Very good with sauerkraut, appetizers, and especially good with oysters.

• Reisling
Very dry, unlike Sylvaner. Nice bouquet, delicate fruit, and goes very well with fish, shellfish, and chicken.

BEAUJOLAIS (red)

Among the Beaujolais we recommend the following three:
• Beaujolais-Villages, Brouilly, and Morgon
Very fruity wines with good body and finesse. They go with a lot of food, from fish to meat. Should be drunk cool, at cellar temperature (55–60°).

BORDEAUX

• Fronsac, Montagne-Saint-Emilion, and Lalande-de-Pomerol (red)
The dominant grapes are Merlot and Cabernet Sauvignon. You can either drink these wines young

or old. Very fruity with a lot of finesse. They go
well with red or white meat, cheese, and possibly
some fish (like red snapper).

• Entre-Deux-Mers (white)
Mostly a sauvignon grape, which is better drunk
very young. Has a nice fruity taste; goes very well
with seafood in general.

BOURGOGNE

• Bourgogne Aligoté (white)
Known in France as the muscadet of Burgundy,
which is a simple, fresh, very nice white wine to be
drunk young. It goes well with seafood, salads, and
hors-d'oeuvres. A very simple wine.

• Rully, Mercurey, and Givry (red and white)
You can find them in both red and white. They are
lighter Burgundies that can be drunk very young
but can also be aged. They are gentle, not aggres-
sive, and easy to drink. Some express great finesse.
The Givry and Mercurey are mostly red, while the
Rully is half red and half white. The Givry is known
as the preferred wine of King Henry IV.

• Mâcon-Villages and Saint-Veran (white and red)
Usually white, and generally made with chardonnay
grapes for the white and with gamay and pinot
grapes for the red. They are light and easy to drink.
The white would be drunk mostly with seafood and
the red with meat.

LE LANGUEDOC (red)

• Corbières and Saint-Chinian (red)
Both wines are mostly red, very generous, and high
in alcohol (11–13%). They used to be earthy, rustic

types of wine with a lot of body, very dark, and
tannic. Now they can be drunk young but will age
well for five years.

SOUTHWEST OF FRANCE

• Bergerac (white and red)
The white has a delicate bouquet; it is a soft wine.
The red has more body which goes very well with
game and red meat with sauce. Good fruity taste
and good body. The red could be kept some three
or four years or be drunk young. The white should
be drunk young.

PROVENCE

• Côtes-de-Provence (white, rosé, and red)
The white is a tender wine which will go very well
with fresh seafood or goat cheese. There is also a
rosé wine that, like the white, should be drunk at
55°. It will go well with bouillabaisse, salade
niçoise, or quiche Lorraine. The red, which should
also be drunk cool at around 60°, is very tender and
goes well with leg of lamb and also with cold cuts.

• Bandol (mostly red)
Most of the Bandol that is found in the U.S. is red.
It is a very tannic and generous wine which goes
very well with red meat and venison. It has a very
spicy taste mixed with an aroma of peppers, vanilla,
black cherry, and cinnamon. It can be drunk young
but ages well.

LOIRE VALLEY

• Muscadet (white)
The muscadet is a dry white wine but not green. It
has an open bouquet and is a wine you can drink at

any time of the day. It goes well with fish and shell-fish. It is also a nice aperitif. It should be served at 50–55°.

• Anjou (white, rosé, and red)
The white is a soft wine, not at all acidic. Lately the Anjou producers have developed more red wines, which are generous, full-bodied wines. They go very well with game and red meat. The rosé d'Anjou is sweeter than both white or red and is a very good summer drink with casual meals. It should be drunk cold (50°).

• Touraine (white and red)
We find red, white, and rosé in Touraine. Most of the red wines are light and fruity and should be drunk young but will keep for two or three years. The white wine, which is mostly Chenin Blanc, is dry with normally a light fruity taste.

• Vouvray (mostly white)
The Vouvray also comes from Chenin Blanc. There are two types of Vouvray: one is dry or sweet depending on the year, and the other is a sparkling wine. Both have a lot of character and could be drunk old, but the sparkling one is probably more apt to be drunk young. With the nonsparkling wine one should eat fish or goat cheese. The sparkling is excellent with dessert.

• Pouilly-Fumé and Sancerre (mostly white)
You might find some Sancerres that are red. Red Sancerre should be drunk at 60°. These are very delicate, fruity, spicy, and fresh wines. They are better drunk young. The white is good drunk as an aperitif and with hot entrées of fish. The red goes very well with rabbit or pork.

RHONE (red)

• Côtes-du-Rhône Village
Very fruity, very easy to drink. Should be drunk young. These wines go very well with game and red meat with sauce.

• Gigondas
Very powerful, high in alcohol, well-structured but at the same time a fine wine with the aroma of licorice, spices, and peaches or apricots. They can be kept a long time and they go well with game and venison.

• Côtes-du-Ventoux (red and rosé)
These wines should be drunk young and cool, with good simple food.

Bain marie is a technique where a cooking pan is placed in a larger pan that contains boiling water. This is sometimes referred to as a "water bath." On top of the stove, it is similar to a double boiler. In the oven, it may be any baking pan that is large enough to hold the cooking pan and can be filled half-way with boiling water.

Beurre manie is a mixture of equal parts of flour and butter, kneaded together, and added bit by bit to thicken a sauce.

Blanch means to cook food in boiling water very briefly, then immediately remove it and plunge it into cold water. This makes tomatoes easier to peel and often removes vegetables' strong taste or the smoky, salty taste of bacon and salt pork.

Bouillon cubes can be substituted for stock. The French cubes are equivalent to the large ones available at the grocery stores. They weigh ⅓ ounce each, measure 1¼ inch, and flavor 2 cups of liquid. If using the smaller ½-inch cubes, use 2 for every one called for in the recipes. Dilute in a small amount of hot water before using and adjust the amount of salt, as bouillon cubes contain salt.

Bouquet garni is a combination of a bay leaf, fresh thyme stems, and several stems of parsley; occasionally celery and garlic are included. The fresh herbs are tied together in a cheesecloth bag or with kitchen string and put in the cooking pot. The bag can easily be removed after cooking.

Braise is the process by which food is cooked in a tightly covered container with butter or a small amount of liquid at a low temperature, either in the oven or over direct heat.

Chiffonade is the technique of rolling leafy vegetables, leaves, or herbs cigar fashion, then cutting them crosswise with a very sharp knife into thin strips. When unrolled, the leaves produce long, thin shreds.

Chocolate preferred for these recipes is a high-quality imported dark chocolate, such as Lindt or Tobler. This chocolate assures superior results with the recipes. Always melt chocolate slowly over low heat.

Escaloper is the method of cutting something into very thin slices, sometimes at an angle, to increase the surface area (as in Filet of Sole and Salmon, p. 86).

Heavy cream has been substituted for crème fraîche (called for in the original recipe) in these recipes. You may use whipping (heavy) cream, half-and-half, or even evaporated skim milk when the recipe calls for cream. Crème fraîche is often available at large supermarkets or gourmet shops. It may be used in equal amounts for cream.

Julienne is a method of cutting vegetables into very thin, narrow pieces—similar in size or shape to "shoestring" potatoes. It is particularly effective with carrots, turnips, celery, and the white part of leeks.

Reci Tips are words of wisdom and time savers that have been passed down through cooking generations.

Reduce is the method by which liquids—any juice, stock, or sauce—are reduced in volume through evaporation, usually by cooking them uncovered. This leads to a concentration of aroma and a sauce base. Continuing the process can lead to a gelatin consistency when the liquid is cooled.

Sweating is the method by which vegetables, meats, or bones are cooked, lightly covered, in very little fat over medium heat and give up their juices. To cut down on fat, vegetables may also "sweat" in broth, wine, or water.

"Très Simple" designates recipes that even a beginning cook can master. The steps are simple and direct, but the results are nonetheless sensational.

WELCOME TO FRANCE

A journey through France offers an unforgettable experience of tastes and flavors found nowhere else in the world. I'd like to share with you my personal recommendations for some wonderful restaurants in the regions of France I'm most familiar with: Paris, Burgundy, and the Château Country.

Probably the best tip I can give you when traveling through France and looking for a great restaurant, bistro, bakery, or hotel is to ask the pharmacist. This is something I do each time I'm in an unfamiliar area. The pharmacist has a wealth of information. He knows the area. He is cultured. He usually speaks some English. He has good taste and the funds to afford it, yet he's usually very careful about spending his money. He always seems to know the best values in the area. Simply buy a tube of toothpaste and start a conversation with him. The pharmacist can often be your best travel agent.

Included here are some of my favorite restaurants and bistros, where the atmosphere is always warm and hospitable. If you mention the name "la Madeleine" to them, you're sure to have an instant friend. They are not "tourist places." Most of these restaurants have a fixed price for a complete meal including an appetizer, main course, vegetable, cheese, and dessert. The tip is included in the price. The price for wine and/or drinks is not included. Although prices are always changing, I have indicated whether the restaurant is expensive, moderate, or inexpensive.

Be sure to call for a reservation when making your dining plans. Also, check the hours and be sure the restaurant will be open that day.

If you are telephoning from the United States you must dial 01133 first, then the telephone number. When calling Paris you must first be sure to dial a 1 before the telephone number.

Paris

LE CAMELEON
6, rue de Chevreuse (Montparnasse), 75006 Paris (Left Bank)
Telephone: 1.43.20.63.43
Very good bistro with a real 1920 flavor. Varied wine selection from all over France. Great "TiTi Parisian" atmosphere created by Laurence Martin and Christophe Surrel. Moderate.

L'OEILLADE
10, rue Saint-Simon (beginning of St. Germain Blvd.), 75007 Paris (Left Bank)
Telephone: 1.42.22.01.60
A small bistro with food cooked the old-fashioned way by the chef, Pascal. Great food for the price. Moderate.

LE RUBIS
10, rue du Marché Saint-Honoré, 75001 Paris (Right Bank)
Telephone: 1.42.61.03.34
(No reservations taken; open every day)
A typical "Bar à Vin," open daily for lunch. Great tartines of country ham, cheese, rillettes, etc. . . . and great "Pinards de Pays" (local country wine). Very inexpensive.

LE RELAIS DE VENISE

271 Boulevard Pereire (Porte Maillot), 75017 Paris (Right Bank)

(No reservations taken; open every day)

A unique restaurant with one main course: sliced steak, served with a special sauce and *pommes frites* (authentic French fries). Since they do not take reservations, you should go at 7 p.m. Otherwise, you will have to wait in line. Ask for Lucienne, the owner. If you want to sound more familiar ask for Lucitte, or if you want to sound like one of the family, just ask for Luce. Inexpensive.

AUX CHARPENTIERS

10, rue Mabillon 75006 Paris (Left Bank)

Telephone: 1.43.26.30.05

Very Left Bank atmosphere created by Pierre Bardèche, the chef-owner, who will guide you to his best beef and veal dishes. Moderate.

LE PETIT MARGUERY

9, Boulevard de Port-Royal, 75013 Paris (Left Bank)

Telephone: 1.43.31.58.59

Like a 1920 brasserie restaurant. The Cousin brothers offer several great dishes. Moderate.

En route to Burgundy

LES TEMPLIERS

45290 Boismorand, Les Bézards

Telephone: 38.31.80.01

A one-and-a-half-hour drive from Paris, south on Highway A-6. A seventeenth-century mail stop set in a beautiful park that is covered with flowers and roses. Les Templiers rates two stars in the Michelin guide and is a truly lovely place to stay overnight. Philippe and Françoise Depée will make you feel at home with wonderful food and their attention to details. Chefs Jacques and Fabrice are a great team in the kitchen, creating and preparing many wonderful dishes. Great menu. Expensive. Rooms available.

L'ESPERANCE

89450 Saint-Père-sous-Vèzelay

Telephone: 86.33.20.45

Fax: 86.33.26.15

Two hours' drive from Paris in the country near the beautiful Abbey of Vèzelay. L'Espérance rates three stars in the Michelin guide. The owners, Marc and Françoise Meneau, will guide you to select a delicious meal. (Marc Meneau also owns le Pré des Marguerites listed below.) Superb food and one of the best tables in France. Expensive.

LE PRE-DES-MARGUERITES

Across the street from L'Espérance.

89450 Saint-Père-sous-Vèzelay

Telephone: 86.33.20.45

Same quality of food as found in L'Espérance, but more casual and more affordable. Food is prepared by owner Marc Meneau, who offers a "menu Pellerin." Throughout history pilgrims (*pellerins*) came to the Abbey of Vèzelay; today people are making a pilgrimage to le Pré-des-Marguerites for its fine food and good value. Inexpensive. Rooms available.

LES JARDINS DES REMPARTS

10, rue Hôtel-Dieu, 21200 Beaune

Telephone: 80.24.79.41

Fax 80.24.92.79

Rolland Chanliaud will offer you elegant cuisine ("Cuisine très Raffinées") at a good value in his private home near the ramparts surrounding Beaune and les Hospices, site of the famous wine auction. Moderate.

The Château Country

The Château Country is a two-hour drive from Paris by car on Highway A-10 and approximately one hour by TGV (high-speed train).

AU PLAISIR GOURMAND
2, rue Parmentier, 37500 Chinon
Telephone: 47.93.20.48
Fax: 47.93.05.66
Jean-Claude Rigollet will welcome and entertain you with the warm "bonne humeur" so typical of the wine region. Great wine from the Loire Valley. Moderately expensive.

LA ROCHE LE ROY
55, Route de Saint-Avertin (near Tours)
Telephone: 47.27.22.00
Fax: 47.28.08.39
Alain Couturier will open his château to you. Very warm atmosphere. Great selection of affordable wines. Moderately expensive.

JEAN BARDET
57, rue Groison 37100 Tours
Telephone: 47.41.41.11
Fax: 47.51.68.72
Sophie and Jean Bardet will make your stay very unique with the quality and the refinement of their food, as well as by the charm with which they serve it. Since they are about 100 yards from my parents, I'm not sure which one is in the shadow of the other, my mother or Jean Bardet. The restaurant rates three stars in the Michelin guide and has a beautiful park nearby. Expensive. Rooms available.

INDEX

Dear Friends,
Thank you for reading this cookbook.
I would like to invite you to experience your la Madeleine French Bakery & Café,
where all the food is inspired by this style of authentic French country cooking.
Merci,